THE RESPONSIVE UNIVERSITY

THE
RESPONSIVE
UNIVERSITY

Restructuring for High Performance

🎓 🎓 🎓

EDITED BY
WILLIAM G. TIERNEY

THE JOHNS HOPKINS UNIVERSITY PRESS
BALTIMORE AND LONDON

07 06 05 04 03 02 01 00 99 98   5 4 3 2 1

The Johns Hopkins University Press
2715 North Charles Street
Baltimore, Maryland 21218-4319
The Johns Hopkins Press Ltd., London

LIBRARY OF CONGRESS CATALOGING-IN-PUBLICATION DATA
The responsive university : restructuring for high performance / edited by
   William G. Tierney.
        p.   cm.
   Includes bibliographical references and index.
   ISBN 0-8018-5715-5 (alk. paper)
   1. Education, Higher—Aims and objectives—United States. 2. Education,
Higher—United States—Administration. 3. Universities and colleges—United
States—Planning. 4. Educational change—United States. I. Tierney, William G.
LA227.4.R45   1998
378.73—dc21   97-37718
                                                                      CIP

A catalog record for this book is available from the British Library.

CONTENTS

ACKNOWLEDGMENTS

I appreciate the help that Syan Ekwegh, our secretary in the center for Higher Education Policy Analysis at the University of Southern California, and Patrick Dilley, my research assistant, provided in the compilation of the book. Jackie Wehmueller, my editor at Johns Hopkins, has been a trusted friend, colleague, and adviser throughout this process. My copy editor, Clive Leeman, has been, as always, first rate. Support for research for part of this book has come from the Pew Charitable Trusts. The Trusts are not responsible for the ideas in the text. Royalties for this book will go to the American Indian College Fund.

THE RESPONSIVE UNIVERSITY

On the Road to Recovery and Renewal: Reinventing Academe

WILLIAM G. TIERNEY

🎓 🎓 🎓

FOR AS LONG AS I HAVE BEEN PART OF THE ACADEMIC ENTERPRISE, colleges and universities have been in a state of crisis, decline, or stagnation. As an undergraduate at Tufts University from 1971 to 1975 I was not aware that I had joined a declining organization, but the pundits, policy analysts, and scholars had already begun to predict our demise. By the time I entered graduate school in 1980, academe appeared to be on death's doorstep. My adviser at Stanford University, Lewis B. Mayhew, published *Surviving the Eighties* (1979) as a manual not necessarily for robust health, but rather as a way to forestall academe's trip to the organizational graveyard. Future colleagues of mine at Penn State University prophesied more academic misery by suggesting that the catchwords of the eighties would be "reduction, reallocation and retrenchment" (Mortimer and M. Tierney, 1979). Now that we are in the 1990s and I live in California, I read the dire predictions of Patrick Callan and his colleagues (Callan and Finney, 1993) about how unprepared the state government and public universities are to handle the multiple problems that confront them. The governor even needs to proclaim a state of emergency for postsecondary education, suggests David Breneman (1995), in a manner akin to what happens when a hurricane rips through the Florida or Hawaiian coasts or an earthquake rolls across California.

The prescriptions for survival have largely been suggestions for better management. Managerial buzzwords and their acronyms—efficiency, effectiveness, MBO (Management by Objectives), zero-based budgeting, adaptive strategy, TQM (Total Quality Management), CQI (Continuous Quality Improvement), responsibility-centered budgeting—litter the academic landscape. Colleges and universities also have been called on to do different tasks and approach old tasks in different ways: We are told we need to do a better job of assessing our students, for example; increasingly, faculty are expected to do less of what they have come to think of as central to their role—research—and more of what they often do not know how to do—serve the larger society. Presidents are supposed to be less philosophical and more adept at fund-raising. We are told we can "do more with less" or, at least, "cut out the fat."

Some critics, such as Roger Kimball (1990) and Dinesh D'Souza (1991), have been shrill, attributing academe's demise to lazy or ill-willed individuals; the faculty often come in for a great deal of blame, with senior administrators a close second. Others, such as Michael Cohen and James March (1974), have not assumed any malfeasance on the part of administrators or faculty; we are simply out of control—"blind men on a freeway," as William Moore suggested at a time when he could get away with forgetting that women might be sightless as well (1971). Managerial remedies have been suggested to help administrators and, to some extent, faculty improve the academic enterprise. No elixir, alas, has proven to be the magic potion for curing academe's ills. MBO, TQM, and most other managerial suggestions have come and gone, and still academe is proclaimed to be weak and in ill health.

To be sure, any organization as tightly tied and fiscally dependent to the external environment as a postsecondary institution will most likely not be in good health if the larger environment is also ill. The tourist industry does not boom in an ailing economy when individuals do not have money to spend for travel. Retailers do poorly during the Christmas holidays in a sluggish economy. Similarly, colleges and universities, especially public institutions, have not been able to maintain or return to robust economic health when they have encountered shrinking federal and state budgets. Few individuals, however, predict that postsecondary education will ever see the rapid period of growth and prosperity that took place after World War II, regardless of the health of the nation's economy. One might well wonder if academic decline will not become a state to climb out of, but a way of life in the twenty-first century. We look to the auto industry, for example, and see how they were ill and now are healthy.

Conversely, we also look at companies that once were healthy, then declined, and have since gone out of business. Whither academe?

The focus of this book is on that question. We neither propose magic pills to cure academic ills nor suggest that decline is a permanent state of affairs. Rather, we suggest that the changes that are needed are more than the sum of the parts. That is, instead of a managerial fix that seeks to reform this or that part of the organization, we argue that fundamental changes need to occur. As we see it, many of the managerial approaches that have been advocated—management by objectives, responsibility-centered budgeting, and the like— may well help improve a specific activity. Such suggestions, however, have not solved the endemic problems that plague the academic enterprise. Colleges and universities have been beset with suggestions for how to treat one or another illness rather than focusing on how to ensure that we no longer get ill. We have been trapped by our assumptions.

Accordingly, we suggest that if academe is to go to the root causes of our problems, we need to rethink and, of consequence, restructure what we do. Change ought not to come from around the edges, but rather go to some of our core activities. We can see that many previous managerial remedies were more concerned with improving systems that already exist than with inventing new ones. While we do not argue with system improvement, our intent here is different, less instrumental and more strategic. Instead of improving a system that exists, we want to challenge old ways of thinking and acting in academe by proffering suggestions about new ways of thinking, and hence acting, in postsecondary institutions.

In the ensuing chapters we have three goals. First, we aim to be deliberately provocative. If we are suggesting that colleges and universities restructure themselves, then we hope to challenge readers with different ways to think about academic roles and rewards. We appreciate the seriousness of the task; our suggestions are neither whimsical nor off-the-cuff. Although we surely do not seek the language of invective or polemic that fills the work of a William Bennett or an Allan Bloom, we also do not write from the detached stance of dispassionate observers. Dramatic change calls for accessible prose and compelling language.

Second, we intend to offer strategic ways for the academy to act rather than merely produce a philosophical tract arguing that times are bad, change is needed, and institutions must find a "vision." In effect, we aim to develop plans for generating internal responses to external demands and constraints.

Third, we keep the focus of the book on systems and structures, rather than on people and personalities. Too often in hard times we look for academic heroes who might lift us up out of the morass, or we seek the villains we think are responsible for this mess. "Leadership" becomes the battle cry of Boards of Trustees in search of a fiscal saviour, or members of faculty who are often unsure of what they want but who know that the present fellow is not a "leader." Undoubtedly, every organization has a few individuals who might be worthy of adulation or blame. Our assumption, however, is that most organizational workers attempt to do their jobs to the best of their abilities. The problems—and the solutions—lie not in individual acts of courage or ill will, but in the structures that frame how we act.

College and university participants have long defined their work in terms of teaching, research, and service. In large part, the focus of this book is tied to a discussion of these areas. We do not so much suggest that colleges and universities depart from these activities as reconceptualize them. Thus, in Chapter One, Ellen Chaffee discusses how postsecondary institutions might become more customer driven. Universities traditionally organize themselves primarily for the purpose of preserving, transmitting, and creating knowledge. We do not suggest a change in such a core function. However, successful businesses have shifted their emphasis from profits to customers. This chapter proceeds from the premise that colleges and universities would do well to shift their emphasis to customer service and satisfaction while they preserve, create, and transmit knowledge. Chaffee argues that the significance of knowledge production will always remain paramount for the academy in the same way that business cannot ignore profit. Chaffee, a college president of two public universities simultaneously, suggests, however, that postsecondary institutions would do well to restructure themselves toward purposeful customer service.

Some readers will have a visceral reaction when we equate "student" with "customer." Others will be able to see how the business enterprise of the organization might be more customer driven, but will reject the idea that teaching and learning should be capital

driven. In this light, long lines during registration are anticustomer /
student, but what takes place inside the classroom, as well as out-of-
class learning activities, has little to do with customers and everything to do with students. Chaffee argues, however, that too often we
forget the "consumer" in the classroom either by scheduling classes
at ill-advised times, not providing prompt feedback when a student /
client / customer has a problem or complaint, or not becoming actively engaged in satisfying them.

Chaffee also seeks to stretch our imaginations so that we consider ways for those of us in academic organizations to think of the
multiple customers we serve—the state, parents, unions, businesses,
students—and begin concentrating more on service to the public
and less on disengaged actions by an academic priesthood. Such a
thesis goes to the heart of what we mean by academic restructuring,
and leads to the arguments I make in Chapter Two.

We do not quarrel with past practices. There may well have been
a time when a college or university served the broad citizenry well by
disengagement and contemplation. The idea of a faculty as a priesthood which removed itself from society in order to think about Truth
is not a notion that should be idly dropped or discarded. Indeed, any
such dogmatic suggestion about a system as diverse and decentralized as the U.S. postsecondary educational one will undoubtedly provoke multiple responses. However, we argue that all organizations,
roles, and functions change over time and context. If service once
meant removal from society, then we argue that today such service
by the faculty might be defined more as direct action, communication, and involvement with society. Rather than assume that we
know what is good for the citizenry, we argue that we need more engagement with society to determine needs, actions, and direction.

Thus, in Chapter Two, I discuss ways to think about faculty productivity. In particular, the chapter focuses on three ideas: (1) academic freedom, (2) faculty roles and rewards, and (3) promotion and
tenure. Just as Chaffee wishes to maintain knowledge production as a
central tenet of the academy, I argue that academic freedom for all
faculty needs to be protected and enhanced; I also discuss the structural relationships in which academic freedom is embedded. I suggest that we need to develop alternative ways to measure productivity and that promotion and tenure might need to be reconfigured.
Simple-minded calls for a faculty to demonstrate more concern for

teaching when the reward structure does not change is futile. I offer alternatives to the current system and suggest that faculty work in the twenty-first century will be quite different from that of this century if we are to keep pace with the needs of society (Tierney, 1993; Tierney, forthcoming).

The first two chapters thus work from similar perspectives and look at what are arguably the two most important constituencies in academe—students, or "customers," and faculty. On the one hand, we argue that how we think about one constituency needs to be reinterpreted; on the other hand, we suggest that how we reward the second constituency for what they do needs to be reconsidered. As we discuss these broad themes, we hope to point out a direction, but not provide a step-by-step Baedeker on how to get there. Our system is too diverse to outline the specifics of how a particular institution would implement a greater concern for teaching, for example, or redistribute internal resource allocations to reward one activity and not another. However, we point out the redirection that needs to be set and suggest that individual institutions rethink what needs to take place in their own organization's cultures and structures.

Making assumptions similar to the ones I make in Chapter Two, Larry Braskamp and Jon Wergin rightfully point out, in Chapter Three, that faculty roles and responsibilities have always been in flux. National priorities on defense and engineering-related issues during and immediately after World War II concentrated the energies of faculty in many disciplines. Nevertheless, the basic categories in which faculty participated—research, teaching, and service, with the emphasis on research—have calcified over the last generation. Ernest Boyer's work (1990) and ensuing books and monographs (Tierney and Bensimon, 1996; Rice, 1996) have generated a good deal of discussion about how we might rethink and change reward structures.

In Chapter Three, Braskamp and Wergin add to this dialogue by outlining the character of new relationships. In effect, if Chaffee argued that we need to think of our clients as customers, and I suggested that we need to redefine faculty priorities, then in this chapter we learn about who some of these key customers are and what one priority for faculty might be. The authors argue that although the core activities of academic life should remain the same, the manner in which we interact with society needs to change. They suggest that instead of being ivory towers, colleges and universities should become community-based conduits for societal change and improvement.

Rather than simply point out what academe's participants ought to do, Braskamp and Wergin, by way of a modified case study, offer concrete suggestions about what needs to happen, and they highlight the challenges and difficulties. In particular, they suggest that education writ large needs to become more integrated and coordinated, instead of existing in isolated segments where parents do one form of training, schools do another, community agencies yet another, colleges and universities another. They argue that postsecondary institutions in general and urban public universities in particular should use teaching, research, and service as a way to improve metropolitan educational opportunities. Undoubtedly, pitfalls exist. Members of faculty often do not think of their audience in a way that promotes dialogue; professors may not have the experiential knowledge to get involved in a "hands-on" approach that is necessary for successful community engagement. Reward structures provide disincentives rather than encouragement. In large part, this chapter takes into account what Chaffee and I argue, and then the authors point out ways to deal with additional problems that they have uncovered en route to creating new institutional compacts.

Roger Benjamin and Steve Carroll's chapter ties the ideas and suggestions from the first three chapters together with regard to institutional fiscal accountability. In particular, the authors suggest that external demands and constraints have created unique environmental contexts so that tinkering with fiscal and decision-making systems will no longer suffice. We need greater accountability, they argue, and decisions that are made in a more rapid, participative context. Benjamin and Carroll first discuss the vertical, departmentally based decision-making structures that have occurred in the past and then posit that such hierarchical chains of command are outmoded and antiquated for at least two reasons.

First, academic arrangements where schools and colleges are isolated from one another belie the latest advances in interdisciplinary thinking that necessitate collaboration and ongoing communication at all organizational levels. Second, technological advances have made information-sharing easier, and hence, imperative. Electronic mail, voice mail, and the like have facilitated communication across campuses in ways that would have been thought impossible only a decade ago. Thus, whereas only a few individuals at a senior administrative level once may have been privy to information, we now face a situation where multiple individuals and groups are able to share in information and decision making simply by the transferring of electronic files.

By no means do the authors intend to suggest that merely by having more information or more communication will academe's participants solve their problems. In this light, more is not necessarily better or worse. More is different. As with the volume's other authors, they argue that "the existing governance system in higher education cannot effectively cope with the problem of reallocating resources." They then go on to offer suggestions for how to reformat the governance structure.

Chaffee, Braskamp, Wergin, and I each concentrate on a particular constituency or issue, diagnose the problem, and argue for a specific solution. Benjamin and Carroll's frame of reference is what many would define as the underlying dilemma in postsecondary education: money, or the lack thereof. They offer a compelling case that academe's resource base is shrinking and, with it, our ability to deal substantively with "real-world" problems such as deferred maintenance or technological upgrades; but more importantly, they argue that the manner in which we make decisions about how to spend these shrinking dollars is inadequate.

When we combine their work with that of the previous chapters, the portrait of academe for the twenty-first century can be seen as an enterprise vastly different from the conventional one of this century. As Kent Keith points out in the text's conclusion, in our desire for rethinking some of our most commonly held assumptions, the authors have created an organization dramatically unlike the staid college and university campuses that once existed. To be sure, vestiges of our past remain. Academic freedom is reinforced. Research, teaching, and service are mainstays of academic work. Institutional sagas will still help define and differentiate institutional types.

What will have changed is how we think of students and who we define as our constituencies, our "customers." The role of the faculty members, their rewards and their responsibilities, will be altered if not entirely different. And governance will be more decentralized and localized, if one accepts the premises of Benjamin and Carroll's argument.

What remains to be discussed is how external environments, especially the state, will function in such a changed atmosphere. Peter Ewell provides an answer in Chapter Five. Ewell points out that in the recent past, relations between state legislators and state higher education commissions and their institutions have been anything but cordial and helpful. More often than not, both parties have claimed intransigence and misunderstanding on the part of the other; fiscal shoot-outs have occurred over one or another appropriation that have left virtually everyone feeling wounded. Put simply, state officials have fewer dollars to spend and desire changes but are not sure what those changes should be. Academic leaders need more money, do not want outside interference, and recognize the need to change, but similarly are not sure what to change or how to do it. One does not have to be a organizational psychoanalyst to recognize that such a relationship is in trouble, with state officials and university leaders speaking past one another.

Ewell does not seek to lay blame on either the state or the institution but instead argues that both parties need to recognize the validity of their often competing demands, as well as the changing nature of relations between state and academe. As do the other contributors to this volume, he assumes that the fiscal constraints that have beset us for a generation now are not temporary. No longer can legislators, collegiate administrators, and faculty deal with one another as if the problems among us are caused by temporary shortfalls of income. In this respect, Ewell echoes Benjamin and Carroll's call to dramatically change the nature of relations vis-à-vis governance, fiscal accountability, and decision making. Whereas Benjamin and Carroll focus on internal relations, however, Ewell speaks of external structures and lines of authority.

The solution, or at least the scaffolding for a solution, lies in a clearer directive from statehouses about what they expect of postsecondary institutions, and more leeway for academic leaders to implement changes. In Europe, for example, technologically advanced countries increasingly have coherent industrial policies that delineate what the government expects from different sectors. Such an idea would most likely be fanciful on the federal level in the United States given that most direct institutional money derives from the state, not from the federal government. Ought we not to expect the setting of some kind of direction for a state's economy that gives participants in postsecondary institutions a sense of where state leaders see the state moving, how they see the economy taking shape, and what role colleges and universities might play?

Ewell is not recommending the often intrusive micromanaging of institutional activities. Such actions are counterproductive, he claims, and most often do not accomplish what has been desired. Thus, rather than oversight, his chapter argues that the state should provide direction and reward behaviors. Just as Benjamin and Carroll call for a more concerted effort at change across a single institution, Ewell suggests the same kind of efforts need to occur across institutions statewide. The state's role, in part, is to facilitate and reward such crosscutting functions.

I suspect that at least three criticisms might result from reading this book. Some readers may wonder why we have chosen to concentrate on one topic (internal resource allocation, for example), and not another (governance and authority roles for boards of trustees). Other readers may find the language jarring or the concept fanciful—"nice idea, but it could never happen at my place"—we might hear. A third reader might accuse us of being philistines suggesting sacrilegious changes in the monastery. Obviously, we would disagree with these observations but would nevertheless acknowledge the authenticity of these critics' concerns.

The first criticism that our choice of topics is narrow recognizes that academia faces multiple problems in many different arenas at present. We could indeed have written a chapter on boards of trustees, technology transfer, unions, the federal role in student aid, affirmative action, and any number of other pressing topics. However, we have sought a unity of issues that, we hope, make up a coherent, cogent argument about how those of us on college campuses might proceed to deal with issues such as technology transfer, student aid, and faculty-administration relations. Simply stated, the stitch work of the text ties topics together to help us think systemically about restructuring the enterprise. The chapters are linked by a coherent sense of the need for dramatic change and a willingness to offer plausible options.

The second and third criticisms about fanciful concepts and philistinism are perhaps more troubling. I noted at the outset that many previous criticisms of academe have often used the language of polemic: faculty members are lazy, administrators are slothful, students are apathetic. Our assumption is the opposite. Most people want to perform to the best of their ability, but the structures in which they work complicate rather than enhance that possibility. We also honestly believe in the essence and import of the academy; it is with this belief that we suggest these changes. The intent of this text is to discuss the structure, offer alternatives, and engage readers in a dialogue so that they might reflect about changes in institutions where they for the most part spend most of their lives. The language here is meant to motivate and stimulate, to move us away from confrontational dialogues about why we cannot change and toward discussions about what we might become as we move inexorably toward the twenty-first century.

References

Boyer, E. L. (1990). *Scholarship Reconsidered: Priorities of the Professorate*. Princeton, N.J.: Carnegie Foundation for the Advancement of Teaching.

Breneman, D. W. (1995). *A State of Emergency? Higher Education in California*. A report from the California Higher Education Policy Center, no. 95-2. Santa Monica: California Higher Education Policy Center. February.

Callan, P. M., and J. E. Finney. (1993). *By Design or Default?* A report from the California Higher Education Policy Center, no. 93–4. Santa Monica: California Higher Education Policy Center. June.

Cohen, M. D., and J. G. March. (1974). *Leadership and Ambiguity: The American College President*. New York: McGraw-Hill.

D'Souza, D. (1991). *Illiberal Education: The Politics of Race and Sex on Campus*. New York: The Free Press.

Kimball, R. (1990). *Tenured Radicals: How Politics Has Corrupted Our Higher Education*. New York: Harper & Row.

Mayhew, L. B. (1979). *Surviving the Eighties*. San Francisco: Jossey-Bass.

Mortimer, K. P., and M. L. Tierney. (1979). *The Three "R's" of the Eighties: Reduction, Reallocation, and Retrenchment*. AAHE-ERIC Higher Education Report, no. 4. Washington, D.C.: American Association for Higher Education (ED 172 642).

Moore, W. (1971). *Blind Man on a Freeway*. San Francisco: Jossey-Bass.

Rice, R. E. (1996). *Making a Place for the New American Scholar*. New Pathways: Faculty Careers and Employment for the 21st Century, Working Paper Series, no. 1. Washington, D.C.: American Association for Higher Education.

Tierney, W. G. (1993). *Building Communities of Difference: Higher Education in the Twenty-First Century.* Westport, Conn.: Bergin and Garvey.

———. (forthcoming). *Reengineering Colleges and Universities: Creating the High Performance Campus.* Thousand Oaks, Calif.: Sage.

Tierney, W. G., and E. M. Bensimon. (1996). *Promotion and Tenure: Community and Socialization in Academe.* Albany: State University of New York Press.

1

Listening to the People We Serve

ELLEN EARLE CHAFFEE

🎓 🎓 🎓

ABOUT FIFTEEN YEARS AGO, AT THE NATIONAL CENTER FOR HIGHER EDU-cation Management Systems, my colleague Rich Allen and I had long collegial discussions in which we made each other more and more furious about management fads in higher education. We decided to blast them from the scene with a scathing and irrefutable article. We identified PPBS (Planning, Programming, and Budgeting Systems), MBO (Management by Objectives), and strategic planning as the best recent examples of those fads. My role was primarily to find facts, and Rich's was to analyze them. Moving toward the conclusion, we were stunned. The paper was never published and I have not seen it for years, but I still remember how we put it: although the first two fads had passed and the third was only beginning, we concluded that all three had "a positive residue of thought and action" that, we agreed, was helping to improve higher education management.

Strategic planning has had more staying power than we would have predicted. And, among others that might be cited, we have seen a new fad that seems already to be on the wane—variously known as Total Quality Management, Continuous Quality Improvement, or simply quality management. I regret the passing of this one, which I attribute primarily to misunderstanding. I believe in it because it represents and extends everything I have learned about effective management from my own research, practice, and observation.

Whatever range of opinions may exist about quality management, I believe that we will look back some day and detect that it, too, left a positive residue of thought and action, including greater appreciation for frontline faculty and staff, greater utilization of their talents, more awareness that you can't get good results from bad processes, and more reliance on facts when dealing with problems. We may then realize, too, that quality management came along at the right time to boost higher education's emerging commitments to student-centered learning and assessment and to help us deal with public demands for accountability.

Central to many of these effects and to quality management itself is the concept of customer focus. *Customer focus* is a common term with an uncommon meaning, the misunderstanding of which may be the single greatest contributing factor to the ebbing of quality management. The purpose of this chapter is to discuss the meaning of customer focus and why we should ensure that it, too, will have lasting impact. I begin by locating it in the context of public demands for accountability from higher education.

Accountability

The demand for accountability in higher education may have begun as a whisper in the 1960s with questions like, "Where does the money go?" "Which college is most efficient?" The public may have been the first to ask, but many inside higher education were curious, too. By 1968, a consortium of insiders had established the National Center for Higher Education Management Systems (NCHEMS), charged initially with developing standard data definitions regarding finances, enrollments, and staffing. At about the same time, the federal government began collecting statistics from every institution in an initiative known first as HEGIS (Higher Education General Information Survey), now as IPEDS (Integrated Postsecondary Education Data System).

We have been far less responsive to escalating public and government demands for accountability since that time. Throughout the 1970s and 1980s, we have tended to respond in ways that conveyed messages like, "Trust us, we're the experts," "How dare you," "What we do cannot be measured," or "We're different." An exception, and perhaps the only significant response, has been the assessment movement. About a decade into it, we are seeing serious efforts to assess student learning on a widespread scale, primarily because of recent accrediting agency requirements. To the credit of our enterprise, this movement is largely generated and led by those within higher education, and we have chosen the most difficult yet important area in which to hold ourselves accountable.

For the most part, however, we have dealt with accountability demands slowly and painfully. We bear an unfortunate parallel to the health care industry, in which doctors, like our faculty, know best, and the claim is that more quality inevitably costs more money. Neither governments nor the public have been as tolerant of that dynamic in health care as they have been in higher education to date. Cost controls such as Diagnostic-Related Groups and third-party review of treatment are well established in health care. If we wish to avoid their counterparts in higher education, we would do well to seize the initiative and embrace the opportunities that accountability can provide.

The first step in preempting outside intervention lies in telling the public what they want to know—or what they should want to know. This is not guaranteed to eliminate concern, but avoidance only escalates the concern. It makes us appear disdainful, fearful, disinterested in public opinion, or uninterested in our own results.

However, questions from the public are often not entirely what they seem. We need to understand and respond to the underlying issues, not just the question. Sometimes questions reveal the effects of false information or assumptions, or a lack of understanding. Recent inquiries into faculty workload, for example, are couched quite understandably in terms of credit hours and class size. Our immediate objection to these inquiries asserts the significance of research and service. Where we have responded, we have done so as if the questions were to be taken literally. We have counted and reported hours and students to show "faculty productivity."

What we seem to find, though, is that the public is asking two questions in one. Faculty workload and faculty productivity are not the same thing (Johnstone, 1994). While some people may literally believe that faculty who mow their lawns on Tuesday afternoons are working too few hours, others have a deeper question. Numerous studies, widely cited, show that faculty work far more than forty hours a week. That such studies have not quelled the public's challenge certainly suggests that there is more to the matter. Credit hours, class size, research grants, and service hours can reveal productivity only on the most superficial level. Productivity is measured best in terms of results achieved. The public would not be so concerned about faculty workload if they were persuaded that students learn much in college and do well in their first post-collegiate jobs, that services add value for clients, and that research yields knowledge with important social or economic benefits.

Offered faculty workload studies, the public is not satisfied. They ask more questions. And those who provided the initial answers wonder in frustration when the badgering will cease and resolve not to waste precious time providing more answers. Failing to understand fully the public's concerns, we create a vicious circle of dissatisfaction.

The public wants cost-benefit analyses that reveal the relative value of each institution and the value of the industry to society (Massy, 1996). Benefits are results to the client not effort by the service provider. Moreover, the public wants benefits not only in the content of educational services but also in their form, with features like convenience and responsiveness. Granting the importance of the "cost" side of the equation, this chapter focuses on the "benefits."

Accountability requires that benefits be defined in terms that are important to the public, and the public must know about them. If a state university gets millions of dollars for research on topics that are irrelevant to the state, sheer revenue may not be enough to generate a sense of benefit among the taxpayers. If the topics are relevant and the results important but the public never knows about it, the institution will never achieve the full value of the research.

Dissatisfaction with higher education goes beyond the general public and is often more implicit than explicit. Student retention to graduation, except for transfers made necessary by programmatic needs, is the single best indication of student satisfaction for those whose goal is a degree. Given that definition, anything less than 100 percent retention indicates an array of problems. These may include lack of appropriate guidance in selecting the institution, lack of appropriate career guidance, inadequate treatment while enrolled, or inadequate financial planning. At the institutional level, the overemphasis on enrollment figures as an indicator of success creates unfortunate incentives that can work against providing student-centered assistance in making a college decision.

Another growing problem is hidden within that definition—the emphasis on a goal of degree completion. If it is true that soon adult workers will need the equivalent of one year of college every seven years in order to keep up with or change careers (Dolence and Norris, 1995: 7), it is impractical to build the college experience almost exclusively on the assumption of a degree-seeking student.

Another dissatisfied group is potential students and their families. Although they may not direct their frustration with the difficulty of selecting a college at the higher education enterprise, we could help them by providing additional information and guidance. Except for basic information such as programs offered, size, and price, we provide potential students with very little assistance in understanding how to select any college or discovering which one holds promise for them.

When the public became increasingly dissatisfied with American automobiles, they turned to Japanese automobiles. A reasonably open market will eventually provide alternatives that respond to public frustration with the current products and services. Higher education is no exception. Accredited for-profit postsecondary institutions like DeVry Institute, based in Chicago, are increasing in number and enrollment. Corporations spend more on in-house training than is spent on all of public and private higher education, and some are beginning to seek accreditation for their schools. Rapidly emerging technologies that bridge distance give such institutions huge potential markets at an affordable price with the added public benefit of convenience. One may already earn a master's degree at a distance from National Technological University in Denver, Colorado. It will not be long before one may earn a baccalaureate degree via technology without ever leaving home, but traditional higher education is unlikely to be the first to offer it.

No institution can satisfy everyone, nor ought it to try. Past efforts to define mission, role, and scope respond to that fact, but usually more from an institutional or industry point of view than from the public's point of view. We need a new approach to defining mission, role, and scope—one that begins and ends with what the institution's relevant publics want, need, and expect from the institution.

Between the beginning and the end, institutions must apply expert judgment on almost every issue, including the definition of "relevant publics"; but their judgment must be applied to the questions that the public is really asking, not what the institution wants the public to ask, and sometimes not even literally to the public's wording of the questions. Nevertheless, the only way to discover the right questions is to listen to the institution's publics. The future of public and private higher education will be very different from its past, and the survival of many traditional institutions could be determined by how willing they are to confront and respond to the public's concerns—to be accountable, in the fullest sense, to the people we serve. Those who are persuaded, as I am, that demands for accountability are now a permanent feature in the higher education landscape will find in "customer focus" the approach and tools to address those demands.

Customers: The People We Serve

In business and industry, the term used for *public* is *customer*. The only reason to create and maintain a formal organization like a business or university is to perform functions that someone—a customer—needs which cannot be done alone or in small groups. A primary definition of what is needed is what customers are willing to pay for, which is determined by their resources and priorities. Competing demands for both public and personal funds are rising rapidly; the costs of operating a university are rising rapidly; and the economy is reasonably steady. This is a recipe for disaster in any industry unless customer satisfaction is rising rapidly.

Responding to customer needs is not a concept new to higher education. Researchers write proposals to address a sponsor's guidelines. Institutions offer academic programs in part because there is sufficient enrollment demand to make them viable. Community colleges and others have industry advisory councils to ensure appropriate career preparation through the curriculum. A premise of this chapter is that customer responsiveness is practiced in and appropriate for higher education, but that we have not embraced the concept with sufficient insight, speed, or thoroughness.

Three great barriers to acceptance have proven nearly insurmountable. The first is the word *customer*. Many in higher education are offended by the term or simply find it inappropriate. The second is the complexity of the concept as it applies to higher education. The third is the complexity of our relationships with our customers.

THE WORD CUSTOMER

Customer, client, purchaser, and consumer are not fully interchangeable terms. A client is one who seeks professional counsel, such as the sponsor of specific research or customized training. A purchaser is one who pays for goods or services. A single college student often represents several purchasers, including self, family, federal and state governments, and scholarship benefactors. Consumers are end users. Students consume higher education as individuals, but society, employers, and families are also consumers of the benefits of their education in the form of better decision-making, skills, and attitudes.

Customer is a more generic term that may encompass all of these. Elsewhere (Chaffee and Sherr, 1992) I have used a substitute phrase, "the people you serve," in part because people in higher education prefer a more altruistic, less commercial term than *customer*. Many are not comfortable with the use of business terminology because it seems impersonal, uninspiring, and selfish. We feel we have a higher calling. The language of families feels more comfortable to us than the language of business. Our perception of business may be inaccurate or unjust, but perception is reality.

Faced with a term they don't like, many in higher education have rejected the concept entirely. Yet the same altruism that often motivates the rejection is also the foundation for the following claim: they would embrace the concept if they did not reject the word. They are in higher education to do good things for people. For some, like those whose primary motivation is the learning of each student, doing good things for people is a well-defined and direct activity. At the other end of the continuum are those whose primary motivation is the discovery of new knowledge that may have no apparent short-term applicability in the world. Many researchers are very articulate, though, when pressed about their motivation—they clearly expect that the new knowledge will lead to good things for people, however long-term, intangible, or unexpected those benefits may be.

Using "the people you serve" or similar language avoids the negative connotations of the word *customer*, relates to a pervasive motivation in higher education, and has the added benefit of making clear the intent behind "customer focus" as that phrase is used in quality management. The intent is that people in organizations should focus on the people they serve. I use both interchangeably here in the perhaps vain hope that eventually they will come to be seen as synonymous. However, in situations where people object to the word *customer*, I use a different term.

Focusing on the people you serve is a prescription with far greater implications for change than may be obvious, as the following simple but profoundly significant examples illustrate. Colleges and universities express their purpose for existence in their mission statements. Consider these actual and typical examples:

> The College's mission has two fundamental and interrelated components: The provision of the highest quality education and dissemination of new knowledge.

> X State College is a public, comprehensive, land-grant institution serving [the state] and the nation. . . . Its mission is the provision of instruction, research, extension, and other public service programs for all segments of the population to achieve their . . . goals.

Statements like these start with "what we do" and sometimes eventually get to "who we serve." They often say more about the institution's programs, activities, and values than about the needs of the people they serve.

Contrast such statements with a small but growing number of exceptions, those that focus on the intended benefits to the people they serve. One is from a newly formed national organization:

> The Council for Higher Education Accreditation will serve students and their families, colleges and universities, sponsoring bodies, governments, and employers by promoting academic quality through formal recognition of higher education accrediting bodies and will coordinate and work to advance self-regulation through accreditation.

The statement identifies the people to be served by CHEA, apparently in priority order, and identifies "academic quality" as the intended benefit. The authors could have been even more precise if they had been clearer about how CHEA's attention to academic quality is supposed to benefit people. For example, they could have indicated whether they intended to protect academic consumers from educational malpractice or promote more effective and efficient learning experiences. The statement concludes with what the first set of mission statements has as its primary consideration: what the organization does to achieve its purpose.

Similar examples from higher education include the following:

The mission of X State University is to prepare students to be learned men and women who [list of six expected outcomes].

The mission of X College is to serve diverse communities of learners who seek intellectually stimulating educational programs which embrace a values orientation and foster ethical development.

Or, if a college were to adapt the mission statement of Great Plains Software, the result might be:

The mission of X College is to improve the lives and personal success of our students, associates, and the larger community by providing superior learning opportunities in the liberal arts and sciences.

The distinction between these two kinds of mission statement is subtle but significant. Both sets usually address both activities and people served. The difference is in emphasis—which is figure and which is ground. It matters. The first set says, "We got together so that we could do some things." The second set says, "We got together because we want to help people in defined ways by doing some things." If the people in each institution were to express their altruistic intentions in their mission statement instead of concentrating on their own activities, they would adopt the second approach. If they were to act on those intentions, they would be pursuing customer focus. Therein lies the irony of rejecting "customer focus" on the basis that it is insufficiently altruistic.

This is not to say that universities fail to help people because they state their missions backwards. The point is that if helping people lead better lives became our primary, conscious motivator, we would change eagerly and in many ways. If freshmen learn better in small groups with a sense of community, why would we do it any other way? If business defines responsibility as the primary need in new employees, why would we make the learning of responsibility a side issue? How could we cling relentlessly to a residency requirement if its benefits are undocumented and it denies some people the opportunity to learn? The very idea that the highest quality courses or majors are those that flunk out the highest number of people becomes patently absurd.

Understanding our mission as helping people lead better lives brings unexamined assumptions to the fore in a process quite similar to what many experience when they realize they have unwittingly been socialized into sexist or racist behaviors. We can see things we never saw before; we become restless to shed old habits that contradict our new insights.

COMPLEXITY OF THE TERM

The second reason that the concept of customer focus is difficult to accept in higher education is the complexity of defining and setting priorities among the people we serve. To illustrate, consider the community college, which may be the most straightforward case.

The primary role of a traditional community college is to provide relevant instruction for people in a defined service region. A secondary role is service, and scholarly research is not normally an acknowledged function. Community colleges exist to help the people there learn what they want and need to learn. The primary customers of instruction are current students and potential students in the region. Eventual consumers include employers in the region, the senior institutions to which students may transfer, and people in the region who use college services. As purchasers, the citizens whose taxes and private contributions help fund a public community college and its students are also customers. Their elected representatives in the state legislature or city council are customers, too. Thus, even in the simplest case, a college has numerous kinds of customers whose wants and needs are diverse. The college may appropriately change its priorities among them over time, and units within the college will find some kinds of customers to be more relevant than others.

Research universities have the added complications that come with their more complex responsibilities. Research sponsors, corporate research and development units, and people from other geographic regions are among their additional customer groups.

In addition to the complexity of constituencies, we have complex time frames to consider. Some assert that the customer is not the student today, but rather the student in his or her life after graduation. In truth, the customer may be both. Research undertaken today may have a direct relationship to public welfare tomorrow, fifty years from now, or never. The uncertain direction of some activities makes it difficult not only to identify any current customer for them but also to offer any guarantees that there ever will be one or that the beneficiary will capitalize on them as intended. This does not mean that we should cease otherwise justified activities for which we cannot identify a current, satisfied customer, but we ought to know what compelling interest justifies them.

Faced with the task of defining and setting priorities among their customers in such a complex situation, many in higher education throw up their hands. This seems unusual in an enterprise that devotes itself to understanding complex things. Instead of devoting ourselves to understanding the phenomenon, though, we leave it to the marketplace to determine who we serve. Let students vote with their feet. Let enrollment decline be the signal of low quality. Bigger is better. Alternatively, let exclusivity or price represent quality. In such circumstances, the good schools are those whose enrollment is growing, those that admit only good students, or those that charge high prices. Not one of these factors is directly related to the quality of the learning experience or the competence of the graduates. Perhaps public demands for accountability on those matters represent increased public sophistication about the false premises under which they had been operating before.

Serving people requires two essential ingredients: a service and someone who wants or needs it. Our orientation has been that we provide certain services and anyone who wants or needs them is welcome to come get it. Many of them, especially those who are fresh out of high school, take their need of a college education on faith— they often are not sure why they need it. They believe it will get them a better job, and it may be required to get the kind of job they want. But their movement through the curriculum takes on a compliance orientation. They do what they need to do in order to get certified, whether they see a connection between what they are doing now and what they want to do later or not.

Older students, however, are increasingly aware of and vocal about their expectations. To the extent that this orientation comes to prevail, institutions that take little interest in student expectations do so at their own peril. If we do not meet student expectations, someone else will. Consistent failure to meet expectations leads to institutional decline. But since we cannot meet everyone's expectations, we need to understand whose expectations are important to us. So we come full circle to the need to define and set priorities among our customers.

In addition to setting priorities among customers, we can determine whether some expectations are common to multiple kinds of customers. If so, these expectations should clearly take high priority. A small public baccalaureate open admissions college in a rural area may serve young students of diverse ability levels, often from small towns or farms, and also displaced farm adults seeking second careers. It may work with local economic development and business groups. Other customers of such a college may include both urban and rural taxpayers. Do these disparate constituencies have any expectations in common? All may expect an affordable cost. They may expect graduates to be competent and economically productive, preferably in terms of in-state job opportunities. For a clientele such as this, the development of self-confidence in graduates may also be expected to some degree by all constituencies. Colleges that define shared expectations are able to simplify the complexity of customer needs among diverse clienteles. The task of setting priorities among them remains, of course, but many expectations such as these are neither mutually exclusive nor intrinsically time-consuming. Some relate more to how the college performs and treats people in the ordinary course of business, rather than how people spend additional time and energy.

COMPLEXITY OF RELATIONSHIPS WITH CUSTOMERS

Without students, institutions of higher education do not exist. Because students are essential and because our viewing them as customers raises numerous complications, this section focuses on students to illustrate complexity of relationships. One may make the case that students are consumers, raw materials, or co-workers, for example.

Although students are consumers, often they are not the primary purchasers of the services they consume as individuals. The state is the major purchaser of collective services in most public institutions, buying down the cost to each student. Other purchasers include benefactors, the federal government, and students' family members. The fact that few students pay the full price, or even the "list price" (advertised cost of tuition and fees, plus associated expenses) of their college education may have major effects on their behavior as customers and therefore on institutional behavior. When we pay for a car, we have two incentives to act like customers with respect to the dealer—one is the pain of the expense, and the other is the fact that we can usually observe tangibly and quickly if something is wrong with the car. If we feel that we paid an exceptionally low price for the car, the bargain may make us more tolerant if we have problems with it. Both the expense and the observable nature of problems are incentives for customer behavior that are diluted in the student-university relationship. Students seldom pay full cost, cannot always recognize a breakdown when it occurs, and find it difficult to compare experiences among universities as they do among cars. Therefore, institutions have lacked one of the primary causes of responsiveness in business organizations, which is that customers complain or quickly take their business elsewhere if they are not satisfied.

Some may say that the student is not a customer because most students are not the primary purchasers of their education. Inarguably, however, students do invest another precious and scarce resource—time from their lives. For young people, though, the value of time may also be unclear. Young students may lack a compelling need to make the most of their time. As the number of older students increases, however, we experience more students who value both their time and their money. They are much more keenly aware of the opportunity costs of schooling if they must forgo work time in order to be in school. If they are willing to do it at all, they insist on receiving value as a fair exchange. Such students may help universities hear more keenly the voice of the customer.

At a minimum, students are daily consumers of our services. In this sense, they are inarguably our customers. However, they are unable in many important respects to define their expectations of us, let alone do so in a knowledgeable way. They cannot know what they need to know until we teach them. They cannot know the value of a physics class to their future lives. One of our services is the expert judgment that goes into defining a curriculum. In one sense, then, students are not so much customers as raw material—we succeed to the extent that we are able to add value while they are with us.

While there is truth in this perspective, it also raises the very important question of whether students are or should become competent to define their own needs in some respects. Clearly, students are the only competent judges of the adequacy of certain teaching mechanics such as whether they can see a visual aid or hear the presentation. They can provide useful input on the relative merits of one teaching approach versus another. Faculty members who reject student competence to define instructional content need not also reject the idea of taking an active interest in the students' views of the teaching process.

Students need to become much more competent in defining at least some of their needs, for example selecting a major and a career that are suitable for them. Self-understanding and career selection are not central and defined services of schooling at any level—we treat them as by-products and optional services that require student initiative. Would student learning, the ultimate measure of academic quality, improve if students felt more secure about where they were headed and how college is getting them there? It's a sensible proposition, but not one that has found its way into the strategic plans of many institutions of higher education.

Even more directly related to what we normally see as our core function, students may need to become far more knowledgeable about their own learning styles and how the brain functions. Rather than saying, "I'll never understand this," they would then be able to say, "Could you draw me a picture of how those concepts relate to each other?" or "I need to hear the conclusion first, and then I'll be able to follow the logic." As more knowledgeable consumers, they would become active aides in their own learning process.

Some would claim that students are not customers, they are our co-workers. If they do not work with us, they do not learn. True enough, although the two are not necessarily mutually exclusive roles. If those who take the co-worker position are faculty members, and if they go on to assert that lack of student learning is always due entirely to lack of student intelligence, hard work, or motivation, as some seem to do, those faculty members do not belong in the classroom. The obvious corollary to that point is that teaching makes no difference.

Yet another complexity is that each student experiences a large number of service providers. With respect to faculty alone, a full-time student taking five courses in each of eight semesters could be in contact with forty different instructors. By the time they may have an opportunity to provide feedback to the instructor, normally at the end of the course, it is too late for them to experience any improvements that may result. Offering feedback during the course is risky, since the instructor holds the ultimate feedback tool, the course grade. These dynamics, too, make it difficult for individuals and institutions to receive customer feedback.

The risk of a wrong decision by education consumers is relatively high, and their recourse is relatively limited. Unlike buying decisions in the marketplace, consumers of educational services are unable to make sophisticated, information-rich decisions about which university to attend, so their initial choices involve substantial risk of dissatisfaction. We provide little, if any, encouragement to make trial use of our services, and we do not give money-back guarantees. Few industries enjoy such a forgiving environment.

Often, discussions about the roles of students degenerate into debates or arguments about which view of their role is correct. The position seems to be that if students can be seen as raw material or co-workers, or if they are incompetent to define their academic needs, then students must not be customers. The logic behind the idea that anyone plays just one role, or that one may assume a role only if one is competent at it, is elusive. However, even those who take this position could be encouraged to consider whether students are among the beneficiaries of university activities, or whether students are among the people they serve. If the response is affirmative, that is all that matters for the present discussion. The rest is semantics.

That a university continues to attract students, that students rarely complain or boycott against individual faculty members, let alone the entire university, cannot be taken as an indication of student satisfaction. It means that the situation is complex and unlike business in some important respects. It means that universities are handicapped in any efforts they make to improve because they do not get full, true signals from a vitally important consumer group. It means that those who take customer focus seriously must make special efforts; they will learn things that may surprise them.

What Can We Do?

In the discussion that follows, I concentrate almost entirely on students and instruction as our primary customers and service. In almost all cases, parallel points can and should be made with respect to research and its clients, employers, taxpayers, benefactors, and other customer groups. In the interest of brevity, that exercise is left to the reader. The section begins with a sampling of actual examples of inadequate customer focus. Suggestions on creating an environment in which such incidents are unlikely to occur address first individual opportunities, then institutional activities and culture. The section concludes with some ideas for collective action.

DO WE REALLY NEED IMPROVED CUSTOMER FOCUS?

Yes, we really do need improved customer focus, although this need varies considerably among universities, departments, and individuals. The following cases illustrate the need:

— Students spend hours waiting in lines and must dash from office to office in order to register for classes.
— Students enroll in classes for which they already know the material.
— A group of rural school administrators asks the graduate institution across the state to provide a distance-delivery program in educational administration. The university declines, unwilling to waive its one-year residency requirement.
— A new student learns upon arrival that she has been given false information about her financial aid package.
— Desperate for enrollments, a rural college establishes an off-campus urban program to serve students on federal assistance. Its program has no learning support services and is poorly matched to local job opportunities for graduates.

— Students cannot graduate in the advertised amount of time due to closed classes.

— A university foundation has record-keeping systems that are inadequate to ensure that contributed funds are used for the donors' intended purposes.

— A coach recruits student athletes whose academic abilities or interests are not compatible with the university's expectations or programs.

— Students complete required general education courses with little sense of why they were required or how to use what they have learned.

If any of these examples, or others like them, could happen on a given campus, that university needs to improve its customer focus.

INDIVIDUAL FOCUS ON THE CUSTOMER

In a very real sense, everyone at work in a university is a customer. Students come for services, whether they be academic, administrative, or personal. Colleagues are the beneficiaries of each other's work, from the participants in a meeting to the office which receives documents that have or have not been completed correctly. Whenever someone supplies others with what they need in a way that they appreciate, he or she is providing effective customer service.

For administrative service personnel, this means courtesy, accuracy, and other characteristics found in many basic service training programs. Nearly always, service people want to do a good job and make a good-faith effort at customer focus. Their efforts may be impeded by factors like a client's frustration dealing previously with the institution, or the red tape of the organization. They may receive mixed messages about whether their job is to enforce rules or to serve customers. In addition, new personnel often lack comprehensive orientation and training programs to enable them to provide effective service from the start. These front-line personnel can be among the most critically important in representing the institution to its customers, and they are least able to take action on their own to improve their services.

Administrators serve those who work for them and the people those personnel serve. Perhaps the most important role of most administrators is to make it possible for those who report to them to do their work efficiently and effectively. Administrators control many of the plans, policies, procedures, and resources that either support or impede that goal. Administrators who believe that their role is to control people, rather than systems, need to change if customer focus is the goal of the institution. Instead, they need to arrange the working environment in such a way that people know what is important and are properly equipped with training, tools, and systems that permit them to successfully pursue what is important.

Faculty provide a university's most central services. Applying customer focus in instruction requires frequently soliciting information and feedback from students for purposes such as ensuring appropriate placement in courses, determining student interests and goals, and identifying any problems with the instructional process. Faculty need to address the variety of learning styles individuals bring to the classroom. They need to act on an understanding of what brain research tells us about learning, for example that "facts, skills, and procedures are best learned when embedded in and linked to rich complex experience" (Caine and Caine, 1991: 11). Moving toward this kind of teaching involves a great deal of learning and change for most faculty members, whose tradition may be to lecture, whose orientation may be more toward the discipline than the learner, whose classes may be large, and whose education about teaching and learning may be purely experiential and implicit. However, any movement at all in this direction is the most significant progress a university can make toward better meeting the needs of the students they serve.

In summary, individuals can take some actions to improve their own customer service, but those with the most individual responsibility for overall improvement are the administrators. It is they who are responsible for institutional support systems that can foster and enable customer focus by all faculty and staff; it is they who direct institutional conditions and actions.

CHANGING INSTITUTIONAL BEHAVIOR

The most important first step in any substantial initiative for change is to identify, strengthen, and give visibility to what the organization is already doing that fits the desired pattern. Not only does this capitalize on existing investments for a fast start, but perhaps equally important, it minimizes the sense that change is impossible or that existing activities are not valued. Fortunately, many activities already occur in a number of universities and colleges to help them understand what students want and need. They should be continued, expanded, refined, and used to define and enact improvements. These activities include:

— student course evaluations
— comment cards on student services
— surveys of student opinion
— program advisory councils with industry representation
— needs assessments in the service area
— detailed profiling of students, market research
— assessment of student academic achievement
— analysis of students leaving the institution, and their reasons
— analysis of student course-taking patterns

We need to know our customers in considerable detail, including who they are, why they are here, their expectations of us, what kind of problems they have, where they turn to when they have problems, and what and how well they are learning. We need to understand the diverse types of students the institution attracts. We need to know their critical requirements of us. These will differ to some extent among institutions, and some may surprise us. Early analyses may reveal issues like parking problems or inadequate teaching. More sophisticated work could reveal that students do not know where to go when they have problems. Digging deeper, we may learn that many are lost, whether due to the size of the institution or inability to make appropriate personal decisions.

Episodic quantitative assessments are only the beginning in the effort to understand our students and their needs. Those who have routinely asked departing students why they are leaving can appreciate how scanty, incomplete, and sometimes false the information from some analyses can be. At least two methods are available to expand the effort to understand: more frequent and informal feedback systems, and purposeful conversations with representative students.

The increasing use of classroom assessment techniques (Angelo and Cross, 1993) is a promising development along those lines. Rather than depending solely on end-of-course student evaluations, classroom assessments are effective tools for determining student needs while there is still an opportunity to meet those needs—

throughout the term. Such ongoing feedback mechanisms are needed throughout the institution. As for qualitative assessments, admissions offices can make good use of marketing-style focus groups. Faculty are finding it worthwhile to seek a small group of classroom volunteers with whom to meet regularly to discuss opportunities for improvement in the class.

The second most important focus for institutional improvement is professional development for faculty and staff. For faculty, professional development is often equated with presenting papers at disciplinary conferences. Important as this is, institutions can and must do a great deal to support faculty efforts to learn about learning and teaching. Sponsoring on-campus conferences, encouraging faculty-to-faculty seminars, and organizing student panel discussions on their classroom experiences are relatively inexpensive methods.

Professional development for staff is so rarely provided, and institutions so often send implicit signals to staff that they are less important than faculty, that almost any kind of professional development support for staff can pay high dividends not only in performance but also in morale. A good place to start would be development of effective orientation programs for new staff, which could include written and video materials for efficiency. Tuition waiver programs are helpful, whether staff enroll in classes that are directly related to their work or not—at a minimum, the classroom experience enables them to be more empathetic and better informed about student experiences. In addition, it may be worthwhile to identify and promote courses relevant to staff performance such as the following: courses on creating effective work environments, on technological innovations like e-mail, on budgeting and accounting, on stress management. Faculty members who teach such courses could provide short topical segments periodically at staff meetings or on-campus staff seminars. Private firms are now offering a vast array of low-cost, one-day seminars useful to staff nearby most campuses in the country.

It is not easy to determine customer needs at the institutional level. Customers can articulate some of them, but not all. Even more difficult for the institution is to establish a safe environment in which to practice customer focus. Unless it is safe to raise concerns about how organizational systems are working, the institution cannot improve those systems. As long as systems are ineffective, people cannot provide exceptional service. The rule of thumb in quality management is that at least 90 percent of problems is due to systems, not individual employees.

A few administrators attempt to motivate people by fear. Even where that is not the case, most administrators would be surprised to know the extent to which front-line personnel work in an atmosphere of fear. The culture of most work organizations assumes that lack of adequate performance is the fault of the employee, with an array of options to repair or eliminate employees with problems. Annual performance reviews are often more effective in reminding people of this fact than in providing useful feedback and support for people. Substantial training programs to assist employees in improving their performance are rare in higher education. Most of the front-line service people, those who have the most direct and comprehensive experience to identify problems with customer focus, are those who have the least power to change inadequate systems and the smallest capacity to cope financially with the loss of their jobs. Some options to reduce fear include philosophical and operational changes in the performance review process, appropriate training for supervisors on how to deal with performance problems and how to distinguish these from problems with institutional systems, and the development of systems to act on and celebrate suggestions for improvement.

No university should solicit feedback unless it has a concomitant commitment to act on the results and to let people know that it has done so. It will have a simple barometer of its effectiveness in this area—if people do not see results, they will stop providing feedback.

CHANGING THE CULTURE

One of the more powerful tools available to those who wish to lead changes toward greater customer focus in higher education is their own use of language. A promising recent trend along those lines is the increasingly frequent appearance of the word *learning* in our collective vocabulary (Barr and Tagg, 1995). Along the same lines as the earlier discussion of the two different approaches to defining institutional mission, "education" is what we do; "learning" is what students do. If our goal is student learning, if we think, talk, and write more about learning than about education, we will inevitably become more attuned to the people we serve.

Similarly, leaders can become increasingly respectful of and curious about what students want and need. They can do so not only in their own interactions with students, but also as they talk with faculty and staff about matters of concern. For example, they can ask, "What do the students say about that?" One of the chief impediments to this is that many seem to think that students want only easy grades and parties. They argue against a goal of customer satisfaction, believing that such a goal will dilute academic quality or even undermine the mission of the institution.

Younger students often speak and act as if they want only easy grades and parties, and they may well believe it. But that is a truth that applies only to some and only superficially, a betrayal of everything we know about human development, and a sad commentary on their life experiences to date. Expectation becomes reality. If we act as if we expect students to want to learn and to have good ideas about how they can learn better, they will respond. We can show real interest in their talents and dreams for the future. We can ask them serious questions not just about our discipline areas, but also about their learning preferences.

With this view of the student, the pursuit of customer satisfaction takes on new meaning. We can enter fully into the joy of service and become actively involved in discovering together how to improve the learning experience. We can develop, pursue, and assess achievement of a responsible definition of what "customer satisfaction" means—responsible both to what students say they want and need, and to the canons of our profession.

One of the results that may surprise us is that learning will become fun. We tend to disparage professors whose students describe their classes as "fun." The reaction may derive from the cynical view of what students want and need. We think fun classes must be easy, or have only entertainment value. But learning and fun are not mutually exclusive. Laughter often accompanies the joy of discovery; people often enjoy pursuing a serious interest.

Careful selection and use of key words and attitudes are especially important among those who hold designated leadership and governance positions. Cultures do not change quickly, and they do not change at all without conscious and consistent leadership behavior. Leaders could do worse than to spend much of their day, or much of their governance agenda, asking these questions of those they encounter:

— How well are you meeting the needs of the people you serve?
— How do you know?
— Are you improving on that?
— How can I help?

When questions like these become part of daily life, behavior changes. People cannot answer these questions if they do not know who they serve or what those people need. Good answers to the second question ("How do you know?") would reflect both the extent to which the respondent has asked the people served what they need and the extent to which the respondent assesses customer satisfaction. The third question ("Are you improving on that?") conveys the sense that meeting customer needs is a never-ending quest deserving continual attention, and the fourth ("How can I help?") commits the leader to supporting that quest and helps eliminate fear.

Caring for the People We Serve

One seldom hears any more the once commonplace statement that a college or university is an ivory tower. To our credit, we have made great strides in providing educational opportunities that respond to the personal growth and employment needs of the people we serve. Given where we started, this was a giant step toward customer focus. It is time to take that development to the next stage: caring for the people we serve.

In a caring university, we apply our expertise not only to deciding what programs to offer, but also to ensuring that their graduates are prepared for success in their careers from the first day—based on what it really takes to succeed, not just what our discipline says is important; based on what we really know about the competencies of each graduate, not just on their credits and grades. We help students succeed in their classes, too, by knowing them, knowing the class requirements, and helping them find a good match and address any deficiencies. Teaching methods are diverse, acknowledging different learning styles, and they reflect what we know about how people learn as much as they impart course content. Standards are high, and so are the expectations that students will successfully meet them.

We take students' failure in a course as an institutional failure, whether due to inadequate instruction, an improper match of the course with the student, or inattention to the personal dynamics that interfered with their success. We do not take responsibility for their action or inaction, but we do take responsibility for ensuring that the institution has done everything it can do to support wise and effective decisions on their part. We take responsibility for ensuring that they know our expectations in advance and have a realistic view of their own ability to meet our expectations. If their abilities are inadequate, we either support their efforts to improve or encourage them to go somewhere else. We do so in ways that enhance, not undermine, their self-esteem.

A caring university knows whether it has a large number of "undecided" students and does not leave their major or career selection to gut-level reactions as they sample diverse courses. A caring university knows that everyone needs learning assistance at some point and ensures that support is available. It knows and intervenes if a field is changing faster than the faculty and courses are changing. It knows that the most important legacy it can provide for its graduates, especially in these changing times, is a love of learning and the skills to pursue it wherever they are.

Caring is part of the culture and should embrace faculty and staff, as well. They, too, are growing and learning. Their views need to be valued and their concerns taken seriously. They help define where the university is going and they know how they are contributing to achieving it. They know and conquer fear through having the courage to take appropriate risks, shunning intimidation. When they see something wrong, they figure out together how to change it. They take pride in their work. The university recognizes their contributions.

These descriptions may sound utopian. They may *be* utopian. But they are nothing more or less than the ultimate outcome of a university that increasingly knows and values both the internal and external customers it serves. After conducting dozens of on-site case studies of colleges and interviewing hundreds of people about their experiences there, I came to the following realization: We typically refer to our enterprise as personnel-intensive because about 80 percent of the budget goes to personnel. What I realized was that we are not just personnel-intensive, we are an intensely human enterprise, not just in budgets but in our very nature. We are also a service enterprise—people provide services for other people. We need neither abandon nor dilute our commitment to knowledge in order to embrace a commitment to serving people. Indeed, we would fail to serve them well if we did dilute our commitment to knowledge. We are in the learning business, and learning is the interaction of knowledge and people. It is time for us to pay as much attention to the latter as the former.

Those who elect to follow this path will frequently find themselves without a map. At such times, they could do worse than remember the approach of a small but highly successful western North Dakota cabinet manufacturing firm (TMI Systems Design) which has a short policy manual with only one primary instruction to its employees: Do what any caring person would do. This principle could be applied with equal success to both the worlds of business and of education.

References

Angelo, T. A., and K. P. Cross. (1993). *Classroom Assessment Techniques: A Handbook for College Teachers (2nd Ed.)* San Francisco: Jossey-Bass.

Barr, R. B., and J. Tagg. (1995). "From Teaching to Learning: A New Paradigm for Undergraduate Education." *Change*, 27 (6), 12–26. November/December.

Caine, R., and G. Caine. (1991). *Making Connections: Teaching and the Human Brain.* Innovative Learning Publications, Addison-Wesley Publishing Company, 1991. Quoted in "Learning Productivity," *Wingspread Journal* 18 (3), 1996 (Summer), 9–11.

Chaffee, E. E., and L. A. Sherr. (1992). *Quality: Transforming Postsecondary Education.* ASHE-ERIC Higher Education Report No. 3. Washington, D.C.: George Washington University.

Dolence, M. G., and D. M. Norris. (1995). *Transforming Higher Education: A Vision for Learning in the 21st Century.* Ann Arbor: Society for College and University Planning.

Johnstone, D. B. (1994). "Productivity of Learning." *Crosstalk, Newsletter of the California Higher Education Policy Center,* 2 (1), 11–12. January.

Massy, W. F. (1996). "New Thinking on Academic Restructuring." *AGB Priorities,* no. 6. Washington, D.C.: Association of Governing Boards. Winter.

2

Tenure Is Dead. Long Live Tenure

WILLIAM G. TIERNEY

IN DAYS OF OLD, THE STORY GOES, A KING OR QUEEN WOULD DIE AND THE cry would go out, "The king is dead. Long live the king!" The simple statement conveyed a variety of messages: one person had passed away; another had assumed the throne. The monarchy remained constant. The passing of one individual may have been tragic, but the citizenry expressed support for the inheritor. Such comments were particularly compelling in times of stress when the king or queen died in the midst of great turmoil.

Arguably, at no time throughout the twentieth century has tenure been more seriously under attack than at present, nor has academe ever been in such turmoil. Although tenure, and what it implies, has become a cherished value—the coin of the academic realm—today we hear criticism of it from multiple arenas. Legislators do not understand its necessity. Public critics attack tenure for its ability to populate the academy with "radicals" or at the least with individuals whose services are no longer required because their specialty is outdated or unnecessary to the modern university. Impatient administrators often fantasize about what their institution might be like without it. The public reads reports about how faculty members prefer research and expend little effort in their teaching. No one can hold the faculty accountable, we hear, because professors have tenure; the citizenry grows restive. Private conversations with faculty members often lead them to admit that some of their colleagues are "deadwood" but that tenure prohibits any action that might solve the problem.

This hue and cry has raised a flurry of action. The American Association of Higher Education (AAHE) now sponsors an annual conference on faculty rewards at which scholarly administrators raise serious questions about tenure's worth, and what alternatives to tenure exist. Professional associations such as the American Historical Association develop alternative definitions of faculty work. Foundations have sponsored studies that seek alternatives to tenure. Books are written. The television show *60 Minutes* has even done an exposé that openly mocks faculty and their reward system. State legislatures and college officials try to abolish tenure so that academe can become more efficient, productive, and streamlined. But despite it all, tenure survives.

The thesis of this chapter is quite simple: tenure as we have known it is soon to die. But tenure will remain. If in Chapter One we heard Ellen Chaffee argue for a new terminology that will help us reorient our priorities, then I am ostensibly going to argue for the opposite: the idea of tenure should not be replaced. However, we need to overhaul the tenure system dramatically, and in doing so we will strengthen the tenets under which it came into existence. Like Chaffee, I am suggesting that contexts—political, economic, social, intellectual—change; as they change, the academy needs to reconsider actions, structures, and constituencies.

In what follows, I first point out the historical antecedents of tenure and then discuss the current concerns that have caused us to focus on tenure as an academic illness that needs to be cured. I consider four alternatives that have been brought forth. I suggest that we have misdiagnosed the problem and that the cure is likely to cause multiple other problems. I conclude by arguing that discussions about the abolition of tenure are ill conceived and take us away from solving the problems that actually exist; I then offer alternatives to how we might rethink faculty productivity.

The Rise of Tenure

The ubiquitous presence of a Starbucks coffee shop on urban American street corners makes one wonder how the Starbucks management is able to deal with such explosive growth. A small shop that sold and served coffee in Seattle a handful of years ago now has multiple functions and outlets. Sure, Starbucks still serves coffee, but customers throughout the country now are also able to do their Christmas shopping, buy jalapeno bagels and cream cheese, or use its locales as a meeting place to listen to jazz.

One might have made the same comment at the beginning of this century with regard to colleges and universities. In a relatively short period toward the end of the nineteenth century and at the beginning of the twentieth, U.S. colleges and universities experienced explosive growth, redefinition, and structural elaboration. Whereas a typical college may have had a minister of religion as president and a handful of individuals as his faculty, by 1920 we see that members of faculty were organized into departments; multiple levels of administration had occurred; and what took place on campus—the work of the faculty—had expanded to include research as a centerpiece of academic life.

Whether at a coffee shop or a college, organizational expansion brings opportunities yet also requires adjustments. One such adjustment was the implementation of the tenure system as a means to define faculty expectations. Insofar as our current system is based on yesterday's problems, I briefly review here why tenure came about in the early part of the twentieth century. My point is not simply to offer an abstract history lesson, but rather to remind readers that tenure did not arise on a whim. If we are to abandon or change it, we ought at least to understand its underpinnings. As George Orwell noted: "Who controls the past controls the future." To understand the past helps up plan for the future.

The antecedents of faculty rights and job security existed in medieval European universities, in early American colleges, and especially in Germany in the nineteenth century. However, and more germane to our purpose, in the United States during the early years of the twentieth century we discover celebrated cases littering the academic landscape of professors being threatened with or actually losing their jobs because of disagreements with university administrators or boards of trustees. Such cases propelled faculty rights and responsibilities as key points for discussion in the academy in an unprecedented way. The cases of Edward Ross at Stanford University in 1900, Richard Ely at the University of Wisconsin in 1915, Scott Nearing at the University of Pennsylvania, and Edward Bemis at the University of Chicago are but four examples of individuals who expressed controversial ideas in writing or in the classroom and faced sanction and dismissal (Poch, 1993).

The rights and responsibilities of faculty thus became a central area for dialogue and debate. Ultimately, the idea of academic freedom became the bedrock of academic life. Stated broadly, academic freedom refers to the ability of the individual to study and teach whatever he or she wants to without threat of sanction. When faculty members are asked about academic freedom today, they invariably point out that a Marxist should be able to teach a class in Marxism or publish about Marx without fear of retribution or dismissal. Stated more succinctly, the Supreme Court wrote the following:

> The essentiality of freedom in the community of American universities is almost self-evident. . . . To impose any straightjacket upon the intellectual leaders in our colleges and universities would imperil the future of our nation. . . . Teachers and students must always remain free to inquire, to study and to evaluate, to gain new maturity and understanding; otherwise, our civilization will stagnate and die. (*Sweezy* v. *New Hampshire*, 1957: 250).

The underlying assumptions in this statement are critical to thinking about what we desire of faculty today. The Supreme Court does not want a "straightjacket" on faculty because to do so would imperil the nation; faculty members should be able to study and teach whatever they want because such freedom ultimately helps society. Universities are seen as places that advance understanding; without the professoriate's freedom to stretch boundaries and limits, society is at peril.

Although the First Amendment protected the free speech of individuals, the amendment said nothing about job security, especially within a private institution. Thus, Edward Ross may well have had the right to speak his mind, but his private employer, Stanford University, also had the right to fire him. Indeed, the lack of written faculty rules and contracts at the turn of the century led to the faculty members' inability to control their destiny. If a dean or president did not approve of an individual's conduct or teaching in the classroom, then the individual could be removed, regardless of whether such removal was justified.

Tenure, then, came about to clarify (some would say calcify) academic freedom in higher education. Faculty had multiple responsibilities that pertained to the right of academic freedom. Faculty members had to be honest—for example, they could not falsify data—and they were supposed to comport themselves with dignity. Essentially, however, tenure was seen as the structure that provided protection for faculty to undertake investigations in a climate absent of recrimination and penalty concerning what the individual chose to research or teach.

In what has come to be seen as the cornerstone that defines the relationship between academic freedom and tenure, the American Association of University Professors' Statement of 1940 noted the following:

> Tenure is a means to certain ends; specifically: (1) freedom of teaching and research and of extramural activities, and (2) a sufficient degree of economic security to make the profession attractive to men and women of ability. Freedom and economic security, hence tenure, are indispensable to the success of an institution in fulfilling its obligations to its students and to society. (AAUP, 1985: 143)

The inclusion of job security ostensibly added a final wrinkle to how tenure has come to be seen. In 1900 an individual could be dismissed without a hearing from his or her peers, and today 85 percent of colleges and universities has some form of tenure guaranteeing due process. Whereas a faculty member at the dawn of the twentieth century was able to be summarily dismissed if what he or she studied, wrote about, or taught was at odds with the official dogma of the institution's president, at the close of the century we have a system that protects faculty from such intellectual intrusions, but which has created other problems.

The Fall of Tenure

Today, tenure still enjoys broad support. Despite changes at some institutions (e.g., "stop-the-tenure-clock" provisions, lengthening the probationary period), the broad fabric of colleges and universities in the United States still has a system in place that has existed for half a century (Trower, 1996). Similarly, faculty still support academic freedom and usually cite tenure as its structural protection (McCart, 1991). At the same time, we have seen a dramatic shift in the tenor and dialogue about academic freedom and tenure. Critics of tenure hold positions on at least five different matters.

1. *Fiscal crises.* Tenure rigidifies positions, argue some, so that at a time when an institution needs to be able to reorganize, it cannot. Over twenty years ago, we heard that "tenure imposes an inflexible financial burden upon institutions" (Commission on Academic Tenure in Higher Education, 1973: 13–14). When an institution wishes to shift resources from one area to another today, tenured faculty often make such a movement impossible. As Chait and Ford have observed, "To tenure a classicist is to tenure classics" (1982: 6). Without institutional flexibility, argue some critics, academe will not be able to keep pace with needed societal changes.

2. *Deadwood.* We often hear that tenure protects unproductive individuals so that nothing can be done to remove them. Accountability has become the watchword for how business and industry have responded to organizational improvement. Once a faculty member achieves tenure, the thinking goes, accountability becomes virtually meaningless. "The procedures for ridding the profession of misfits" note Bowen and Schuster, "are so arduous and so embarrassing that few administrators are willing to take the time of themselves and the faculty to prosecute the cases. The procedures take on the flavor of a trial for murder" (1986: 243). Further, in an age when lawsuits to rid an institution of someone with tenure who has not met his or her duties are commonplace, such litigation might end up costing the institution hundreds of thousands of dollars even if the individual's tenure is eventually revoked.

3. *Experimentation lessened.* Rather than protect people so that they might experiment, the rigidification of the system has made scholars risk-averse so that they are assured of getting published. As assistant professors struggle to gain tenure they are more likely to engage in studies that offer "quick and dirty" data leading to immediate analysis and publication instead of studies that may take a longer time period and may not lend themselves to publishable scholarship in time to beat the tenure clock.

Conversely, when institutions tenure someone, the investment is potentially a multimillion dollar decision. "The risk averse university," states O'Toole, "does not want to tenure an individual who makes waves intellectually, who takes risks with new ideas, who thumbs her nose at the conventions of her discipline, or worse, who doesn't fit neatly into any one discipline" (1978: 27). Thus, organizations use tenure as a way to move individuals toward conformity rather than exceptionality. From this perspective tenure rigidifies norms rather than protects the intellectual vanguard.

4. *Untenured not protected.* Tenure only protects those with tenure; the assistant professors, adjuncts, and part-timers do not have protection for academic freedom. Those who are tenure track faculty often need to conform to the whims of senior faculty if they are to achieve tenure. Van Alstyne, for example, noted that "the anxiety of prospective nonrenewal may be seen to chill the appointee's academic freedom in a manner unequaled for those members of the faculty with tenure" (1971: 331–32). In this light, we have unwittingly created a class-based system of haves and have-nots with regard to a principle—academic freedom—that was supposed to permeate the entire institution.

5. *Academic freedom.* Whereas academic freedom was important once, today the need for tenure is less because of legal protections and an enlightened climate. Academic freedom also is a protection that very few individuals actually need; the vast majority of faculty never write or say anything that tests the limits academic freedom is expected to protect. When faculty members have been surveyed about their own needs for academic freedom they overwhelmingly have commented that they themselves have not had a direct need for such a protection (Keith, 1996). Indeed, Slaughter (1981) pointed out that close to 90 percent of the cases that the AAUP investigated pertaining to tenure had to do with issues surrounding financial exigency rather than academic freedom.

The portrait that the critics draw is of an organization with a cumbersome structure that restricts institutional choice and ability to respond to the needs of the day. At a time when the broad public—state legislatures, community groups, families, foundations—looks to the college or university for leadership in solving many of the "real world" problems that confront them, the public finds a professoriate unwilling or unable to respond in large part because of the reward structure that has been put in place. Thus, critics argue, if academic freedom is no longer under attack and there are alternative methods available (e.g., individual contracts) to ensure individual liberty, then why not rid ourselves of an outdated structure? If tenure restricts organizational action, depresses individual creativity, and protects unproductive faculty, then why not create a system that more adequately meets the needs of the twenty-first century?

If we assume the goodwill of the critics of tenure and believe that they have the best interests of the academy in mind, what kind of responses to these five challenges might be forthcoming? Certainly there is a degree of validity in virtually every charge that has been made. Many institutions are under fiscal duress. Unproductive tenured faculty members do exist. Rigid tenure requirements can reduce the desire to experiment. If tenure protects academic freedom, then those without tenure do not have an equal protection. And certainly, the more egregious examples at the turn of the century that I pointed out with regard to violations of academic freedom do not appear to occur on as large a scale today. Furthermore, during the worst of times—the McCarthyite witch-hunts of the 1950s— tenure did not protect many faculty; they were simply dismissed (Schrecker, 1983). However, grains of truth do not imply that the point that is being debated is proved or disproved. Alternative responses also exist.

Fiscal Crises. Tenure does not preclude an institution from acting when it faces fiscal problems, argue tenure's supporters; it only clarifies relationships and responsibilities. During the last twenty years, colleges and universities have retrenched, and tenured faculty have been let go. Surely we should not assume that we want to mirror activities in the current marketplace where thousands of employees are summarily dismissed in order to downsize the organization; a college community implies some form of a social contract with the faculty.

Deadwood. The assumption that unproductive individuals are protected by tenure assumes that organizations without tenure do not have unproductive personnel. No evidence exists that shows that a college or university has more unproductive personnel than a business company; the problem, then, lies in how to increase performance. Rosovsky, for example, has estimated that unproductive faculty are under 2 percent of an institution's faculty (1990: 211). Can a business or other organization boast of a better level? We have mistakenly assumed that an organizational structure—tenure—protects unproductive personnel when organizations without the structure also have the same problem.

Tenured faculty may also be removed, but only with adequate cause. Why would we not want to guarantee in a college community that an individual has a secure job unless there is due cause against employment of that individual? Conversely, tenure may also be thought of as a filter. As opposed to organizations in which no formalized decisions are ever made, individuals are liable to drift in mediocrity throughout a career; at a minimum, tenure sets standards and highlights organizational expectations.

Experimentation lessened. Experimentation for some individuals may lessen, but we also have examples of individuals who had tenure and were able to develop breakthroughs in multiple areas because they had the time that tenure afforded without feeling they had to produce. Similarly, although a tenure system may not be perfect, the alternative that individuals propose—a system without tenure—would not increase the prospects for individual creativity. In the business world, for example, individuals are fired if they do not produce in timely fashion. Tenure at least creates the conditions in which experimentation is possible.

Untenured not protected. True, the untenured do not have academic freedom, but it seems an odd logic that argues that because one group does not have a good, then no one should have it. If academic freedom is important and we need an institutional structure to support it, then some individuals will be protected by the structure—tenure—while others work their way into the structure, and still others remain forever outside the gate (e.g., part-timers). The Commission on Academic Tenure in Higher Education noted that tenured faculty, not fearing loss of their own jobs, "form an independent body capable of vigilant action to protect the freedom of their nontenured colleagues" (1973: 15). From this perspective, the tenured act as guardians of academic freedom within the institution; they are not simply beneficiaries of tenure.

Academic freedom. That few faculty members test the principles of academic freedom today does not mean that it is no longer important. Indeed, there are still plentiful examples of academic freedom being abridged in the late twentieth-century United States (Benjamin and Wagner, 1994). One might also assume that many faculty members in 1900 also did not test the limits of their discipline. An analogy is apt: simply because most U.S. citizens do not test the limits of free speech does not mean that we should abolish the First Amendment.

Similarly, mistakes such as those which occurred during the Mc-Carthy era do not necessarily indicate a fatally flawed structure. Again, the Supreme Court has erred in its judgments many times, but few call for its abolition. Simply because faculty members at a particular institution do not feel threatened today does not mean that a problem may not arise tomorrow. No one could have predicted the witch-hunts of the 1950s, and we of course cannot predict future twists and turns in the political and social climate of the country. Particular rights like freedom of expression reflect the values of the whole community (Benjamin and Wagner, 1994). Academe's goal should not be to abolish tenure because defending academic freedom is no longer necessary; rather, we should strengthen tenure to ensure that academic freedom remains protected.

Although both sides of these arguments have merit, what is troubling is the academic ping-pong we often play as groups talk past one another to prove their point. Indeed, such a problem is particularly worrisome with crucial issues: academic freedom, tenure, productivity. Before changes are proposed, it is certainly important to understand the positions of different constituencies. Most individuals in the academy recognize the need for change, but they cannot agree on the kind of change that is necessary. Our central point is that tenure as a fundamental structure is now facing calls for change ranging from reformulation to complete elimination. In 1950 we saw tenure as the bedrock of academe, whereas today many question its worth if not decry it as the root cause of our problems.

Alternatives to Tenure

In general, one might divide the discussion about tenure into two parts: (1) the strengths and weaknesses of tenure as an employment practice, and (2) the necessity of having tenure to protect academic freedom. Oftentimes, those who see the weakness of tenure as an employment practice disagree dramatically with those who see tenure as a guarantor of academic freedom.

Obviously, more alternatives exist than simply eliminating tenure or maintaining the status quo. When individuals try to move beyond the ping-pong nature of the arguments listed above, a variety of options come into play. In a system as diverse as the one we have in the United States, one would expect multiple alternatives to exist. In what follows, I discuss four possible scenarios, which are the most significant changes that have been proposed and which have gained the most currency in the recent past. That is, they are increasingly talked about and debated as possible alternatives for the future.

CONTRACTS

One might create long-term contracts that are renewable after some form of review. For instance, an individual could be hired for a fixed period—six or seven years—and then be reviewed. The review might occur with at least three different perspectives in mind: (a) Is the candidate's contract worthy of renewal? (b) Is the area in which the candidate teaches and performs research worthy of the fiscal commitment for another long-term contract? and (c) Can the institution afford such a commitment?

Proponents of this idea argue that its strength is that it enhances institutional flexibility, provides the opportunity to downsize academic areas that may no longer be of academic interest, and ensures that academics maintain a degree of scholarly vitality if they want to be renewed for an additional term. In effect, the tenure process that an assistant professor goes through every six years might become the norm for someone's entire professional career. One's academic freedom is also protected by the security of a long-term contract that few other employees in the workplace have.

Another suggestion is that institutions still have a tenure track, but that long-term contracts could be an alternative for faculty who might prefer such an arrangement. An incentive clause could conceivably be provided in which faculty members who chose this option rather than the tenure track (or gave up tenure for a contract) might receive an earlier sabbatical, summer pay, or an early retirement benefit.

Critics of this approach argue that academic freedom is compromised by it in much the same way as if tenure were simply abolished. In addition, such a two-tier arrangement would only exacerbate a system that is already overly hierarchical. The necessity for constant re-evaluation raises the potential problem that the demand for excellence will be compromised while academics constantly look over their shoulders, knowing that who is evaluated this year will be their evaluator next year. As the Commission on Academic Tenure in Higher Education noted, this arrangement could well "lead to mutually supportive mediocrity on the one hand or to factionalism on the other" (1973: 16). This kind of contract renewal could also damage morale and reemphasize that academics need to "publish or perish"; rather than conduct thoughtful work, scholars will only perpetuate the rush to publication. Faculty governance will be weakened, argue the critics, and administrative authority will be strengthened. Others believe that such an evaluation system, if done well, would be unworkable because of the demand for constant, formal assessment measures.

Finally, many of the problems that critics of tenure list—poor teaching, a lack of concern with public engagement, the need for different kinds of work (examples of which will be suggested in the following chapter)—are not addressed in any meaningful way by the move to long-term contracts. In many respects, the critics of this alternative see contracts as creating more problems rather than less because academics will have less job security and incentive to change.

TENURE AND SALARY DEFINITION

In economic terms what tenure really means has never been defined. Recently, some have argued that tenure equals a portion of one's salary, but not necessarily the entirety of it. Until now, the assumption has been that tenure is equivalent to one's salary. However, during the last few years the financial problems that have beset institutions in general, but medical schools in particular, have led administrators to recalculate what is meant by tenure from a fiscal perspective. A professor of clinical medicine, for example, might have a salary of $200,000 derived from several different sources—grants, medical practice, and teaching services. The professor might also have tenure. What portion of salary is he or she due when the university's medical practice dries up because of changes in health care and grants no longer being available?

Some will argue that all tenure line faculty should receive a base salary and an additional stipend or bonus for particular forms of work, with the remainder dependent on the individual's ability to generate income. The argument here is that, for example, when faculty members become department chairs or administrators, their salaries are often increased to reflect a twelve-month contract for additional work. However, when they resume faculty work after a few years, then they should return to their "base" salaries rather than retain monies for tasks no longer performed.

Another alternative would be to set salary levels but provide only a percentage of the individual's salary. Thus, an individual salary may be $60,000 and the central administration would provide the department with the equivalent of 90 percent, or $54,000 of the salary. How the department raises money for each member's additional 10 percent is up to the department. The department members may work together and combine their resources, so that monies from all external grants that generate income, special institutes or seminars where fees are charged, or summer courses, are pooled. An alternative is to have an ideology of "every man and woman for him- and herself."

The practical advantages of these scenarios are almost entirely fiscal. Some proponents will suggest that when a department needs to generate income for the collective, it will experience a sense of camaraderie and singularity of purpose. However, most proponents simply point out the economic advantages, or more likely, the economic necessity, of implementing such policies. They argue that central administrations simply do not have enough resources to support departments, and tenure is a resource-intensive undertaking. Privately, they may also admit that mistakes were made in the past and they have no alternative but to rectify errors of previous administrators. Usually, the "mistakes" refer to the awarding of tenure to academics such as clinical medical professors who did not have hard-line funding, but instead subsisted on grants and contracts to help run medical hospitals. Twenty years ago few individuals could have foreseen the crisis that would exist in health care; these problems have affected universities in a major way and are redefining what tenure means in economic terms.

Criticism of this approach is severe. If one's base salary is so low that it does not constitute a livable wage, critics argue, then tenure means nothing. The purpose of tenure has always been to make academics immune from the vagaries of administrative meddling; when one equates tenure with a percentage of what one receives from the administration, then the importance of tenure is depressed, the role of the faculty is weakened, and administrative power and control rise. Ironically, argue some, the rationale for these changes is based on administrative incompetence in the past. Why, they argue, should administrators be given more power and authority over academic life when their decisions got academe into trouble in the first place?

Academic freedom is weakened when job security is threatened. The idea that a department will pull together when it needs to generate funds assumes that its members will not compete with one another for scarce resources. Critics of this suggestion argue that the more likely outcome is less willingness to work with one another, and a markedly less positive environment overall.

LOCATING TENURE

Perhaps as controversial as defining tenure as part of an individual's salary is the idea of locating tenure in a particular department or school rather than at the general institutional level. Again, the driving force behind this concept is the desire to deal with the fiscal pressures that administrators and trustees feel they are under. A state system, for example, may face budget cuts in the state legislature and decide to close a branch campus with the expectation that salaries will be saved and costs reduced. However, because it is implicitly assumed that individuals work for "the university" rather than a branch campus, redundant faculty members do not automatically lose their jobs; they are redeployed. Of consequence, no savings occur.

Proponents of this alternative point out that unlike corporations where employees may implicitly be given lifetime employment and be expected to work wherever they are needed, colleges and universities offer lifetime employment (i.e., tenure) for a specific task such as teaching and writing about sociology or art history. As McPherson and Winston note, tenure "is a guarantee of employment in a specific set of tasks with well-defined perquisites" (1993: 111). Thus, within a postsecondary institution, there is little ability to redeploy individuals. Once an art history professor, always an art history professor, even if there is no need any longer or if the individual would be better off elsewhere.

The criticism of such a position is again severe. Detractors point out that departments do not declare fiscal exigency, institutions do.

The desire to rid the organization of employees in this manner, argue the critics, makes a mockery of tenure and weakens academic freedom. They also point out that in the vast majority of cases where professors create patent agreements, such documents are signed between the professors and their institutions, not the departments. It is curious, the critics allege, that the institution seeks to establish guidelines and control over an employee in one arena, but in that most basic of actions—tenure—the university now wishes to absolve itself of any long-term fiscal obligation. Finally, once again, the critics point out, tenure becomes the whipping boy for financial problems. The importance of academic freedom is ignored entirely.

POST-TENURE REVIEW

One way to meet the criticism about deadwood has been to propose some form of post-tenure review. The manners whereby individuals might be reviewed are multiple: One possibility is that every individual is reviewed every year and merit raises are decided on based on the evaluation. A second possibility is that all individuals are reviewed periodically—perhaps every three years on a rotating basis. A third possibility is that only those individuals who have been deemed unproductive are reviewed.

When post-tenure review takes place and by whom varies a great deal also, although institution-wide post-tenure review is more the exception than the norm. One sees post-tenure review stop at the department or school level, especially when every individual is reviewed each year. Outside letters of reference or evaluations as rigorous as those which take place for tenure are also generally not required. Again, the reason for post-tenure review is fiscal, although proponents generally point out that academic freedom is in no way threatened by simply evaluating academics who already have tenure.

The response to such a plan is based more on procedure than on philosophy. Many critics are able to envision plans that do not threaten academic freedom, although such plans do nothing to strengthen academic freedom either. The procedural concerns are similar to the issues raised with regard to term contracts. One is that creativity and collegial relationships would be harmed (Wesson and Johnson, 1991: 53). A second concern is that a great number of individuals become involved in the assessment of a candidate for tenure

and such work is done on an entirely voluntary basis. If post-tenure review is to be serious and professional, the critics argue, the workload will balloon out of proportion. If the assessment is not to be rigorous, then why do it? An additional concern is that such a formula enables deans and department chairs to avoid face-to-face, frank discussions with the faculty (Wesson and Johnson, 1991: 54).

Another point of contention is the intent of post-tenure review. If the implicit focus is to revoke tenure, then of course, many academics would reject the idea. However, most proponents of post-tenure review point out that they do not want to change tenure, they merely want to find the deadwood and figure out how to evaluate them. The critics point out that a department or school's faculty members already know who the deadwood are; a post-tenure evaluation appears headed only in the direction of scapegoating individuals rather than solving the problem. "It is self-evident," notes James Perley, president of AAUP, "that the problem of deadwood does not lie with tenure but with institutions that do not honestly evaluate individuals prior to the granting of tenure, that do not ensure help when problems arise, or that do not take the appropriate steps to terminate for cause" (1995: 45).

We see that possible solutions or alternatives can generate as many, if not more, objections as those made by the original critics of the problem. Nevertheless, one might even anticipate from those original proponents of change a guarded affirmation that their critics have a point. Similarly, their critics might accept the basic premises upon which the solutions are devised; colleges and universities do have severe fiscal problems. Thus, well-intentioned and fair-minded proponents of tenure reform often realize that these ideas of a contract system, salary reform, and a redefinition of tenure appointment levels (institution, school, or department) are not optimal. And yet, they ask, what are we to do in economically hard times?

Opponents of tenure reform quite frequently agree that we are in difficult economic times, but they are concerned that we ought not to harm a system that has functioned effectively for much of this century. In effect, then, we have reached a stand-off. Virtually all parties agree that the status quo is unacceptable, but there is no concurrence about what to do.

I do not intend to engage in an act of hubris by suggesting that what follows will calm the waters of academe and solve our dilemmas. Rather, like Ellen Chaffee, I offer here a strategy to think about the problem, in this case, tenure reform. My goal is to provoke us to think about tenure, faculty productivity, and problems such as deadwood, in different ways, and in doing so, enable us to act in a different manner.

The Future of Tenure

In the late-twentieth-century United States we seem to have an obsession with evaluation. The media report SAT scores or institutions' reputational rankings as if organizations are involved in horse races and the purpose is to reward winners and sanction losers. A simple, summative evaluation defines performance. SAT scores are twenty points lower today, we hear, than a decade ago, and we know the schools are doing a poor job. A university's school of education rises three notches in national rankings and the president gives the dean a raise. The dean, in turn, applauds the faculty's effort.

Summative evaluations are helpful. Simple, quick data points are part of what a decision maker needs to arrive at an informed conclusion. If SAT scores have fallen, then an admissions officer, state policy analyst, or freshmen English teacher may well find such information useful. However, too often we substitute summative evaluations for formative evaluation and assessment measures. I agree that faculty members need to be evaluated after they receive tenure. Such evaluations, however, should be formative as well as summative.

In Chapter Five, Peter Ewell offers suggestions about how state legislators and policy analysts might foster what he has previously called a "self-regarding institution" (Ewell, 1984). Echoing Ewell, I argue that an effective, excelling institution will exhibit an overriding concern for organizational processes and goals. Indeed, Ellen Chaffee has charted the way for us to think about students and other "consumers" all being involved in an engaged and developmental process, instead of assuming that the professoriate and administrators know best how an institution should be administered and students should be taught.

Similarly, if academe is a community, then we need to focus on how assessment is an ongoing developmental activity. The discussions move away from getting rid of deadwood or how tenure as a structure is an impediment to change. Instead, we pay attention to improving the culture of faculty life by discussing in depth—honestly, concretely, personally—how we as a faculty, and as an individual, might improve (Tierney, 1993; Tierney, forthcoming). Reflexive assessment moves away from a culture of fear and retribution and toward an understanding of how to create a climate for improvement. In effect, I am suggesting that rather than develop an evaluation system that looks backward and determines how well someone performed, we create a structure that looks forward and tries to outline how the individual and organization want to perform.

In many respects, we find on our campuses today a culture where administrators and faculty are more alike than different in their assessment of others. We develop impressionistic observations of one another; we discover attributes and characteristics of our colleagues that are weak or in need of repair; we then fail to speak with those same colleagues about how they might improve and how we might be of assistance.

To be sure, some individuals relish finding a colleague's weak point and "going in for the kill." I obviously do not endorse that kind of dialogue. But I am also not denying that some individuals either are unable or unwilling to improve and that we will need to deal quite specifically with their assignments and employment. However, those who seek to tear someone down, and those who deserve dismissal, are a minuscule number in any college or university. Indeed, as already noted, no empirical evidence suggests that academe has a higher percentage of deadwood than other nonacademic organizations. If that is the case, then why think of tenure as a problem? The much larger issue pertains to how we create the climate that is necessary for change if what I have outlined in the Introduction is to be believed (see also Tierney, forthcoming).

I am suggesting that targeting tenure as the culprit is a mistake. At the same time, tenure as we currently know it needs to change. A single evaluation point for anyone—much less engaged intellectuals—is insufficient. There is a good deal of evidence that tenure in many cases has protected academic freedom; until we devise a community-wide structure with similar protections, we ought not to do away with it. However, the institution of tenure should not prevent us from moving toward creating a more engaged, productive faculty.

In effect, I am suggesting that we develop a supportive culture that demonstrates to our colleagues that we have obligations to one another. Both Rice (1996) and I (1993) have previously pointed out that academe has arrived at a place where individuals feel isolated from their campuses and colleagues. How might we change? I offer four suggestions that might serve as a basis for change:

FEAR VERSUS ENCOURAGEMENT

The best way to enable individuals to change and improve is through a climate of encouragement as opposed to fear. Discussions about tenure that are framed as if faculty members are obstacles, deadwood, or laggards is unhealthy. Conversely, discussions about ways to help faculty improve and develop help us to define goals for making the individual and the unit (e.g., department or school) mutually supportive of one another. Intellectual development needs to be fostered in academics, not browbeaten into them. Too many previous discussions have been framed in a manner that creates a defensive response from those under attack.

PERSONAL PERFORMANCE CONTRACTS

Over the course of a twelve-month period my life invariably changes. Someone calls me unexpectedly and asks me to write an article that I had not planned on writing but that I would like to try doing. A colleague is promoted, and I am asked to teach her course, one I had not considered. An opportunity arises to work with Native American graduate students in a two-week seminar. And of course, personal responsibilities and crises take turns that no one could have expected. No one is able to chart with 100 percent accuracy how his or her work life will proceed over a twelve-month period; too many contingencies circumscribe our actions.

Nevertheless, we ought to have some form of shared understanding about our goals for the next year and how we intend to reach them. Without such goals our work becomes helter-skelter; a sense of unity and vision within my department or school becomes difficult to sustain; the larger community does not help me attain my goals. One way to develop a shared understanding would be for us to delineate in writing how we envision spending the next academic year. In many institutions, when an academic applies for a sabbatical, such a statement is necessary; I am suggesting we might consider performing such a task not merely when we write sabbatical proposals, but as ordinary practice from year to year.

Personal performance contracts should not be so rigid that they prevent academics from capitalizing on unforeseen opportunities, but they also should be firm enough to provide academics, administrators, and colleagues with markers upon which to base advice and judgment. Thus, in a community concerned with development and quality we have an obligation to outline where we intend to go, and how we intend to get there. If we are to develop personal performance contracts, then our conception of administration and faculty roles and responsibilities should also shift.

THE DIALOGICAL ADMINISTRATOR

I interviewed an administrator recently who said to me: "The problem of tenure is the problem of administration." He went on to state that administrators are too hesitant to sit down and periodically talk with the faculty; instead, they are consumed by meetings and administrative minutia. His assessment of administrators was not meant to be pejorative or cynical; indeed, he was himself an administrator. Instead he was pointing out a common occurrence: formal and informal formative assessment activities do not take place often enough in academe. The skeptic will argue, however, that when an article of mine is rejected by a journal, or I get a poor teaching review, I receive formative feedback.

But the kind of formative assessment I am suggesting has more to do with a frank formal discussion with a department chair or dean about one's performance contract than with a lonely rejection letter one reads in the solitude of the office. In the study by Estela M. Bensimon and me that involved 300 interviews of junior faculty, even for those on the tenure track, we discovered feelings of drift and lack of clarity about what was expected of them (Tierney and Bensimon, 1996). If administrative life is so consumed by meetings and paperwork that administrators are unable to become engaged with their faculty, then we need to change the structure of their workdays rather than make the misguided accusation that tenure is to blame for perceived faculty inadequacies. Honest dialogue about expectations and goals that confronts shortcomings, objectives, goals, and institutional needs in a straightforward manner offers dramatic opportunities for change.

FACULTY GOVERNANCE AND RESPONSIBILITY

When one reviews the literature about tenure and faculty productivity, one finds that the vast majority of the proposed changes are suggested by administrators or policy analysts who see problems—lack of finances—and suggest solutions. The faculty then reacts to such suggestions. As faculty members, we need to be more responsive, proactive, and action-oriented. I am not suggesting that we pile yet another activity on an already busy group of individuals, but if we assume that teaching, learning, and research are important, then we need to build efficient ways to work with one another on improving our work. We currently think of assessment and evaluation as something that is required by external groups; we need to reorient our thinking so that evaluation becomes a defining core activity of what we mean when we say we are an academic community. What do we mean by the term *academic community*, and how does its definition have an impact on the work I do?

One example pertains to teaching. Although there are bright spots on the academic landscape, far too often the assessment of teaching pertains to little more than adding up the cumulative scores of student evaluations. Again, our obsession with summative evaluations reduces teaching to little more than Olympic diving competitions where the individual is able to say "I'm a 4.56. How about you?" If we are concerned about teaching then we might build in dialogical moments during the academic year where faculty members sit in and observe one another's classrooms, not to report and judge to an external authority but as a way to engage in conversation about how to improve one another's teaching.

In the study I did with Bensimon, one question I asked faculty members was whether they thought there was a specific aspect of teaching (e.g., lecturing, grading, leading a seminar) where they thought they could improve. They invariably said yes; they immediately pointed to one part of their teaching with which they were unhappy and wanted to improve. Unfortunately, when asked if their department or college created the culture to help them improve on that aspect of their teaching, they just as invariably said no. If we want faculty members to improve their teaching, then might we not actively work on doing that rather than blaming a structure like tenure? If we do not change the culture in which faculty members work, then tenure's elimination will not improve teaching, although it will erode the protection of academic freedom.

LONG LIVE TENURE

Suggestions of the kind I have sketched here are neither incremental nor easy. Tenure, as we have known it, needs to change in order to keep pace with new social, intellectual, and economic contexts, as do all organizational structures. We ought not to reify a structure—tenure—and assume it is a belief that cannot change; we also should not take a belief—academic freedom—and assume that it can be supported without a structure. Protecting academic freedom as the bedrock of the academy is imperative if we are to remain intellectually curious, competitive, and free. But tenure as we have known it will not be particularly functional for the changed circumstances of the twenty-first century.

Instead, I have suggested an alternative conceptualization of how we might think about tenure. Tenure's basic outline remains. What changes is the culture in which it is embedded. Individual faculty members accept the premise of a performance contract throughout their careers as a way to gauge their progress and enable their colleagues to offer input, advice, and support. Academic administrators reorient their work life so that they are able to participate in formative assessment and evaluation activities. They engage in honest discussions with their faculty about ways to improve and ways for each party to support such action. The faculty members accept their profession as a calling that necessitates particular obligations to one another and to the greater good.

Undoubtedly, some readers of the previous chapter were uncomfortable with Ellen Chaffee's use of the term "customers"; just as surely, some readers of this chapter will assume that individuals work for themselves, that administrators do not have time for dialogue, and that faculty members are too self-absorbed to involve themselves in communal action. I appreciate and understand such thoughts. Ironically, however, the activities surrounding the practice of tenure belie such an interpretation. Each year faculty members involve themselves in the arduous task of evaluating their colleagues either by writing external letters of assessment or sitting on institutional review committees. All of this work is uncompensated. My simple point is that individuals are willing to work for the greater good, but they need a supportive, affirming culture in which to accomplish this improvement in communal action. As Roger Benjamin and Steve Carroll argue in Chapter Four, the road to fiscal stability is through more extensive horizontal—rather than hierarchical—relationships. I have suggested how one such road—tenure—might be improved and made more horizontal; if we follow these suggestions, we will re-create tenure for the twenty-first century.

References

American Association of University Professors (1985). "Academic Freedom and Tenure: Statement of Principles, 1940." In *ASHE Reader on Faculty and Faculty Issues in Colleges and Universities*, ed. M. J. Finkelstein. Lexington, Mass.: Ginn Press, 143–45.

Benjamin, E., and J. Wagner, eds. (1994). *Academic Freedom: An Everyday Concern.* New Directions for Higher Education, no. 88. San Francisco: Jossey-Bass.

Bowen, H., and J. Schuster. (1986). *American Professors: A National Resource Imperiled.* Oxford, England: Oxford University Press.

Chait, R., and A. Ford. (1982). *Beyond Traditional Tenure.* San Francisco: Jossey-Bass.

Commission on Academic Tenure in Higher Education (1973). *Faculty Tenure.* San Francisco: Jossey-Bass.

Ewell, P. (1984). *The Self-regarding Institution: Information for Excellence.* Boulder, Colo.: National Center for Higher Education Management Systems.

Keith, K. (1996). "Faculty Attitudes toward Academic Freedom." Doctoral dissertation, University of Southern California, Los Angeles.

McCart, C. (1991). "Using a Cultural Lens to Explore Faculty Perceptions of Academic Freedom." Doctoral dissertation, Pennsylvania State University, University Park.

McPherson, M. S., and G. C. Winston. (1993). "The Economics of Academic Tenure: A Relational Perspective." In *Paying the Piper: Productivity, Incentives, and Financing in U.S. Higher Education*, ed. M. McPherson, M. Schapiro, and G. Winston, 109–31. Ann Arbor: The University of Michigan Press.

O'Toole, J. (1978). "Tenure: A Conscientious Objection." *Change*, 10(6), 24–31.

Perley, J. E. (1995, January-February). "Problems in the Academy: Tenure, Academic Freedom, and Governance." *Academe*, 81(1), 43–47.

Poch, R. (1993). *Academic Freedom in American Higher Education: Rights, Responsibilities and Limitations.* ASHE-ERIC Higher Education Report No. 93–4. Washington, D.C.: George Washington University.

Rice, R. E. (1996). *Making a Place for the New American Scholar.* New Pathways: Faculty Careers and Employment for the 21st Century, Working Paper Series, no. 1. Washington, D.C.: American Association for Higher Education.

Rosovsky, H. (1990). *The University: An Owner's Manual*. New York: W. W. Norton & Co.

Schrecker, E. (1983). "Academic Freedom: The Historical View." In *Regulating the Intellectuals*, ed. C. Kaplan and E. Schrecker, 25–43. New York: Praeger.

Slaughter, S. (1981). "Academic Freedom in the Modern University." In *Higher Education in American Society*, ed. P. Altbach and R. Berdahl, 73–100. Buffalo: Prometheus Books.

Tierney, W. G. (1993). *Building Communities of Difference: Higher Education in the Twenty-First Century*. Westport, Conn.: Bergin and Garvey.

———. (forthcoming). *Reengineering Colleges and Universities: Creating the High Performance Campus*. Thousand Oaks, Calif.: Sage.

Tierney, W. G., and E. M. Bensimon. (1996). *Promotion and Tenure: Community and Socialization in Academe*. Albany: State University of New York Press.

Trower, C. A. (1996). *Tenure Snapshot*. New Pathways: Faculty Careers and Employment for the 21st Century, Working Paper Series, no. 2. Washington, D.C.: American Association for Higher Education.

Van Alstyne, W. (1971). "Tenure: A Summary, Explanation, and Defense." *AAUP Bulletin*, 57(3), 328–33.

Wesson, M., and S. Johnson. (1991, May-June). "Post-Tenure Review and Faculty Revitalization." *Academe*, 77(3), 53–57.

3

Forming New Social Partnerships

LARRY A. BRASKAMP AND JON F. WERGIN

★ ★ ★

HIGHER EDUCATION TODAY HAS AN OPPORTUNITY UNIQUE IN ITS HISTORY
to contribute to our society. Signs of social fragmentation are everywhere: a lack of hope for a better life, especially for those under
thirty; substantial poverty, especially among our children; moral
decline; the breakup of the traditional family and community; increased drug use and violence in the schools. A larger and larger seg-
ment of our society, people with good academic and career skills, is
unemployed or about to be unemployed. Neighborliness, voting participation, PTA membership, scout activities, and even the number of
bowling teams have been on the decline over the past decade (Putnam, 1995). In short, the civic life of our democratic society has become weaker, and so, some would argue, has our democracy.

By tradition and nature, higher education has played numerous
roles in the life and progress of our society. As the late Ernest Boyer
(1996) pointed out, American higher education greatly contributed
in the early days of our country by preparing civic and religious leaders. In the 1950s and 1960s the academy responded to the national
call to better prepare our students in science to meet the challenges
of the Soviets who sent Sputnik into space. But as Boyer argued, "Increasingly, the campus is being viewed as a place where students get
credentialed and faculty get tenured, while the overall work of the
academy does not seem particularly relevant to the nation's most
pressing civic, social, economic, and moral problems" (1996: 14). The
ivory tower seems often to be above the pain and problems of the ordinary American workforce and its daily hassles. Many educational

institutions have gates, well-manicured lawns, shrubs and flowers, walls and trees to buffer the campus from the outside world. The academy does not often believe and act as though the campus is the world and the world is the campus.

Constituencies are now asking higher education to open these borders. State legislators, employees, professional associations, and federal government agencies are all asking the academy to link work and school and to become more active partners in addressing and solving our social ills and be more competitive internationally. In July 1995 the National Center on Postsecondary Teaching, Learning and Assessment, in conjunction with the Education Commission of the States (ECS), sponsored a national conference on the topic of "Extending the Reach of Reforms in Undergraduate Education." Several governors on a panel discussing the future of education warned that higher education is about to undergo even more scrutiny and criticism. No longer are policy makers willing to excuse higher education while questioning the effectiveness and value of K–12. Policy makers are thinking instead in terms of P–16 (preschool to senior year in college).

A salient theme of our public policy makers (governors; local, state, and national legislators; mayors) seems to be this: the education of our youth is in trouble and all levels of education are responsible for improving it. The call for change is combined with a seriousness about results and local responsibility. Politicians are increasingly questioning the effectiveness of grand, national-scale interventions based on elaborate plans. A decentralized, localized, grassroots approach, involving partnerships of community resources, is receiving increased support (Imig, 1995).

Institutions of postsecondary education and their faculties are expected to become part of these partnerships and offer their creativity, knowledge, and analytical problem-solving skills. To some this is a new development. But in truth, the work of faculties has never existed in a vacuum. Their current research emphasis, for example, is due in part to past national priorities on defense and engineering. The problem is that today's priorities are different. External audiences are asking for a different kind of social relevance from higher education: They are asking it to enhance K–12 education and to better prepare the young for work among other demands. The academy will benefit by recognizing the depth of this concern and joining in the dialogue, both admitting its shortcomings and vigorously defending its unique role in society.

In this chapter we outline the character of these new relationships. We argue that universities and colleges need to reorient themselves as active partners with parents, teachers, principals, community advocates, business leaders, community agencies, and general citizenry. As Donald Jacobs, dean of the Kellogg School of Business at Northwestern University, stated: "The university has got to be closely connected to the public we serve, otherwise the public's going to go in one direction, and we're going to go in the other" (1996: 3). We argue that higher education will enhance its usefulness to society by becoming a forum for critical community dialogues, by advancing practice-based knowledge and policies as well as upholding the creation of theory-based knowledge, and by utilizing faculty expertise in new ways—in short, by forming new social partnerships.

We begin by describing two major programs at the University of Illinois at Chicago that highlight the challenges and difficulties of forming social partnerships. We then suggest that substantial changes are needed in how faculty work is defined, organized, and evaluated to meet the challenges. We end with some suggestions about how academic leaders can help universities become more engaged in our society.

UIC as an Urban Land-Grant University

As a land-grant institution, the University of Illinois at Chicago (UIC) has a long history of commitment to integrating teaching, research, and outreach (public service). In 1993, Chancellor James Stukel, in his State of UIC address, made the university's mission very public by stating that "during the next ten years, UIC must become the nation's leading, urban public research university, striving to accomplish the land-grant mission in an urban setting. In doing so, it will become a much greater participant in the education, cultural, community and economic life of metropolitan Chicago." To achieve this, the chancellor introduced the "Great Cities Initiative," a program to symbolize its previous, present, and anticipated outreach activities, but also its teaching and research activities at UIC.

Great Cities is to be the signature of UIC and to help make UIC a model urban land-grant university. One of the six goals of Great

Cities is "nurturing collaborative relationships with surrounding urban and suburban elementary and secondary schools in order to improve the quality of education in the region." Through its scores of outreach and public service programs over the past several years, the College of Education at UIC has been actively pursuing this avenue of partnership. It has a mission that stresses collaboration with schools and community agencies in preparing teachers and administrators, providing professional development for practitioners, and advancing the knowledge and understanding of educational and child development in urban settings. In short, faculty engagement in K–12 education has reinforced the mission of the university and the college.

UIC's urban land-grant mission in education must be viewed within the context of school reform in Chicago over the past decade. In 1988, the Illinois State legislature passed the Chicago School Reform Act, which stressed the importance of parents, community members, Local School Councils (LSCs), and local schoolteachers and administrators as key forces and influences in school reform. Previous system-wide standards were viewed as leading to centralization of power and authority which was reduced in favor of strong community and parental involvement. Schools were to become community resource centers connecting professional educators with the local community. From 1988 to 1995 school reform in Chicago was a massive experiment in decentralized decision making, based partially on the notion that a student's success is inextricably linked to his or her total learning environment, an environment that includes the neighborhood and the family, as well as the schools themselves.

In 1995, the state legislature passed another sweeping reform bill, giving the mayor of Chicago unprecedented power and control of the schools (Hess, 1996). The mayor was able to pick the five-member Board of Trustees and the CEO, which replaced the position of the General Superintendent. A new management team from city hall, handpicked by Mayor Richard Daley, reflected a political and business rather than an educational orientation (Klonsky, 1996). The issue of centralization and decentralization of power once again became more salient. With strong support from Mayor Daley, those in the central office stressed accountability while the reform groups most often tried to uphold the value of local control through strong and autonomous LSCs. This second phase of Chicago school reform was accelerated because of the new leadership and Mayor Daley's active involvement in the schools and the central authority's prerogative to identify and intervene in nonperforming schools. The theme of accountability through student test score improvement reinforced two of Mayor Daley's statements about the Chicago Public Schools made frequently on television and at public meetings: "I no longer talk about school reform, but of school accountability," and, "All of Chicago must unite behind the children of Chicago."

Two Examples of UIC and K–12 Partnerships

We present brief accounts of two examples of partnerships between UIC and the K–12 school community in Chicago. We admit that these are not typical examples and that they differ from such common partnerships as teacher education, curriculum development, evaluation of interventions, and workshops for school personnel. In both examples, the president of the University of Illinois, Stanley O. Ikenberry, was the initial contact person with the outside world. He supported and took a personal interest in both initiatives. The chancellors of UIC and University of Illinois at Urbana-Champaign (UIUC) were also engaged and supportive. In a sense, the dean of the College of Education was assigned to these initiatives, which blended and reinforced his personal agenda and the college's mission. We present these unique cases because they vividly and starkly illustrate issues, concerns, challenges, and most importantly opportunities for faculties and universities in forming social partnerships.

THE NATION OF TOMORROW

The first of two major partnership programs between UIC and Chicago Public Schools began before the 1993 announcement of the Great Cities Initiative and the 1988 Illinois legislation that produced the decentralized form of governance in the Chicago Public Schools. The Nation of Tomorrow (TNT) program emerged in the mid-1980s at a time when national leaders in higher education and philanthropic foundations began to realize the enormous implications of population shifts to urban America and that higher education was not addressing the growing urban problems. The W. K. Kellogg

Foundation, the principal funder of TNT ($3.68 million), based its support on two expectations.

First, TNT would be designed to enhance the learning and development of young people in Chicago, particularly those who live in communities with a limited enriched environment. The goal was to develop communities of support and to use the school as the critical community developmental center. Faculty at both UIC and UIUC would have the opportunity to gain insight into urban education issues and to develop an integrative social services model of schooling which focused on an ecological approach to education.

TNT was a comprehensive project in four Black and Hispanic neighborhoods, using the school as the focal institution. The project's name was taken from a 1909 speech by President Theodore Roosevelt, who said, "When you take care of children, you are taking care of the nation of tomorrow." The Nation of Tomorrow had four objectives:

1. Improve learning opportunities for children by developing improved teaching methods.
2. Help parents learn how to aid their children's educational development.
3. Increase the availability of high-quality day care and after-school youth programs.
4. Expand school health programs and access to primary health care, for example, health checkups at school, referrals to existing health resources, continuing care and follow-up.

TNT drew on the talents of more than seventy faculty and staff members from the University's Chicago and Champaign-Urbana campuses, including the Colleges of Education, Nursing, and Social Work; the Cooperative Extension Service and the Schools of Kinesiology, Human Resources, and Family Studies; and the Colleges of Applied Life Studies, Medicine, Dentistry, and Pharmacy (Levin, 1994).

Second, the Kellogg Foundation desired to influence a social transformation of UIC as a land-grant university. It provided an incentive for the university to refine its mission, to revise its organizational structure, and to alter its rewards of faculty achievement in ways that would be consistent with an emerging urban land-grant university. The foundation encouraged UIC to reexamine its commitment to the common good and to make appropriate policy and administrative changes to merit this new commitment. In short, this partnership was intended to influence the university's goals and mission as well as to help the children of Chicago.

LOCAL SCHOOL COUNCIL (LSC) TRAINING

The second example of partnership between UIC and the Chicago Public Schools is more recent and differs significantly in its genesis, scope, and the nature of the partnership. In the spring of 1995, the Illinois General Assembly asked the University of Illinois at Chicago (UIC) to help them better understand the Chicago Public Schools (CPS) situation. They desired a "neutral" assessment of the status of CPS. During the legislature session in 1995, UIC faculty members and the dean of the College of Education served as consultants to some of the legislative leaders, for example, the chairperson of the House Committee on Education. In their role as consultants, they stressed this theme, "The overarching design problem for stage two of Chicago school reform is how to strengthen both the central authority and the local school simultaneously" (Braskamp and McPherson, 1995: 1). During the end of the session, the legislature asked the Chicago area universities to become even more engaged in school reform by organizing and providing training for 6,000 local school council members. The law read, "Training of local school council members shall be provided through Chicago-area universities at the direction of the Dean of The College of Education at the University of Illinois at Chicago and in consultation with the Council of Chicago-area Deans of Education. Incoming local school council members shall be required to complete a three-day training program provided under this Section within six months of taking office." UIC agreed to help because this leadership role reflected its Great Cities mission—to use teaching, research, and public service to improve the quality of life in metropolitan areas.

UIC immediately organized a Coalition for Local School Council training involving universities, school reform and community organizations, and educational organizations, including the Chicago Public Schools, to plan and implement the training. Throughout the fall of 1995 this coalition of more than fifty members wrote and pilot tested six three-hour lessons on the roles and responsibilities of LSC members, school improvement planning, budgeting, and principal selection and evaluation. As chair of the Coalition, the dean of the College of Education at UIC stressed a common theme of the lessons—mutual accountability based on student learning. Since accountability became a very public issue in this phase of reform, no one community or reform group wanted to publicly argue against the emerging message from the Mayor's Office that everyone—universities, reform groups, Chicago Public Schools, parents, communities—must collaborate to improve student learning. It also meant that the focus of training was to be on improving student learning and not on school governance or local politics, which had become the main issues in many controversial LSC battles since 1989. Power struggles between the local school principal and the LSC members no longer were considered an effective way to reform schools.

The theme of mutual responsibility also forced the local school councils to realize that, as leaders, they too were responsible for student learning. The LSC members could no longer place blame on the principal or teachers and fire the principal if they did not like what they saw. In fact, more than 80 percent of the principals holding office in 1995–96 were hired in the last three years and were thus hired by many of the local school councils.

LESSONS LEARNED

These two programs have provided UIC faculty members and administrators with sufficient experiences to offer some observations on the challenges of forming new social relationships between universities and other organizations dealing with children. (It should be noted that the UIC College of Education annually has about forty externally funded projects under faculty supervision and leadership that involve partnerships.) We offer these observations.

Faculty members are not accustomed to the messiness of direct engagement in societal problems. In the LSC project, faculty members were often uncomfortable with the messiness of the situation, the conflicts, the explicitness of power struggles among the school reformers and Chicago Public Schools' central administrators, the direct intervention of Mayor Daley in school reform, and the local press's extremely and unusually positive portrayal of school reform. The arena was one of partisan struggles for specific outcomes and some faculty members felt that they neither fitted nor belonged in such an arena. They valued the role of recognizing all sides of an issue and promoting ongoing study and debate, while non-university participants pressed for closure and implementing decisions made rather than prolonging debate and study.

The school reform groups who campaigned for reform in both 1989 and 1995 initially viewed local universities as too elitist and too unconcerned about Chicago school reform, only becoming involved when foundations provided funds for research and intervention programs. In the first months of LSC training, one reform leader commented, "Why have the universities been given this responsibility? They are seen as elitist here, whereas training should be a grass-roots process" (Pick, 1995: 30). University faculty and staff, particularly those who strongly identified with the established research university perspective, did not feel they deserved public criticism for their new venture in helping others.

Faculty members often lack experiential knowledge of the issues being addressed. In both the TNT and LSC projects, most faculty members quickly learned that their knowledge of schools and reform was not very deep and insightful. In discussions with reformers, they discovered that their analyses often seemed like naive textbook answers to those in the fray. The faculty members had analytical knowledge based on surveys and statistical analyses but often could not match the horror stories and insights of reformers who had spent all their time in the larger community of schoolteachers, principals, parents, policy makers, businesspersons, and citizens. But many faculty members became quick learners, while others withdrew to their former work.

Faculty engagement in social partnerships creates major personal and professional challenges. Faculty members who became involved often felt a profound impact, even though at the time many of the experiences were painful and uncomfortable. One faculty member recalled, "TNT brought on a revelation in my own thinking. And it enhanced the kind of research that I wanted to do. Initially it was motivating inner-city African American students to do writing. But now it's branched out to more, what they call critical education in terms of how young people can look at society and identify who they are in that society, and think of ways of empowering themselves to deal with their situation" (Confidential communication to Larry Braskamp). Other faculty members in TNT realized that their involvement would not produce tangible results like publications, but that their involvement was more personal. In another confidential communication to Larry Braskamp, one stated, "My willingness and interest in continuing is, I think, a personal commitment to the teachers more than anything else. I felt that this was a tested enough opportunity to see how we could function as an urban university." Another made the following point:

> If the university only relies on a traditional definition of research, then projects like TNT will not exist. Thus, I mean even the questions change. The questions themselves have to emerge from the community. The researcher, the academic person, has to be able to go with it in a very committed, long-term way, and to report in such a way that doesn't violate the process that's happened. You can't twist it into a traditional research approach when it wasn't traditional to begin with. And then there has to be some outlet for that research to allow the faculty member to be successful [as an] academic. It's an odd marriage. (Confidential communication to Larry Braskamp)

Other faculty members indicated how they were personally affected by the TNT experience, such as hearing first-hand personal accounts of child abuse, and the fear of working in the midst of violence. These were stories coming from children they worked with, not from reading a book in the library. Some also felt that they were changing the attitudes and behaviors of teachers. One commented, "I see a lot of the work I do as planting seeds" (Confidential communication to Larry Braskamp).

For those faculty members who remained involved with TNT throughout the five-year period, some were not always comfortable because they were not educated in urban schools or had little or no prior experience. They did not know how to conduct research with very little control over their projects and with very little advanced planning. In short, it was too much "action research" for them.

Faculty members involved in LSC training became tired of the continual "in-your-face" mentality and the need to negotiate everything. For some, the conflict between both fulfilling academic standards of excellence in writing the training materials and making them politically and educationally useful to local citizens surpassed their own sense of academic excellence. Nevertheless, in both cases, faculty members learned that developing highly integrated and complex partnerships required a set of conceptual, social, and professional skills different from those provided by their traditional training. They thus developed a greater appreciation for the problems of inner-city schools.

Universities and schools both have bureaucracies that limit the nature of collaboration and cooperation. The university's bureaucratic structure and that of the schools at times added up to a very cumbersome and inflexible impediment to conducting productive business. In TNT, some of the community advocates who were ideal candidates for the type of work required (e.g., they were from the community and knew the community well) could not pass the university civil service job requirements. University rules did not provide a user-friendly atmosphere; instead, principals saw roadblocks and more promises than reality. The university was cast as a difficult collaborator.

In the LSC partnership, the university initially took responsibility for writing the content of the program, training the trainers and making all the necessary administrative arrangements, such as locating sites for training, signing up LSC participants, monitoring attendance, and paying for child care and food for the Saturday training sessions. The administrative arrangement proved costly, cumbersome, and inefficient. One large bureaucracy handling administrative details for another one produced too many barriers to accommodate last minute adjustments in the schedule. For example, the dean of the College of Education had to use his personal credit card to purchase the Saturday lunches and get reimbursed later. Major administrative changes were later made and the Chicago Public Schools became responsible for finding sites, notifying LSC members of the training sessions, and monitoring attendance. As one faculty member stated, "Universities need to focus on what they do best—educate."

Collaboration does not occur without the partners spending time together to foster mutual trust. Cultures of local schools and reform organizations differ in significant ways from a research university and the clash of cultures had to be dealt with continuously. In TNT, individual professors initially ran projects of service which integrated their own research, but later faculty teams tried a cross-disciplinary approach. In the LSC training project, faculty members had considerable difficulty adjusting to the political posturing of the reform members and the perceived lack of a code of conduct for group decision making. Faculty members were often asked to switch from being educators—writing the lessons or training instructors—to being strong and vocal advocates of Local School Councils. They could not stay above the fray between community special interest groups and the CPS central administration. One reformer wanted to use "the clout of the university" in battling the central office over the role of LSCs in school reform. Not taking sides was difficult, but both the central administration and the reform community eventually came to regard the university community as the most neutral, objective, and focused of the participants.

In both programs, social capital—networks, norms, and trust between members to achieve a common good—initially did not exist. It had to be built over time, over many meetings. There was little "we" at first, but gradually trust and reciprocity occurred in both projects, taking months and years, not days or weeks. Even then the trust was fragile and could never be taken for granted. However, trusting relations did form in the LSC training program especially, and they became significant and often personally very meaningful to the partners whether they were from UIC, CPS, or a reform organization. In work sessions which, one year later, lasted several hours, the participants from UIC, CPS, and the reform community often laughed together and commented on how far they had come in the process.

The LSC partnership was formed and sustained in a most unusual context—the partnership was mandated by law. All parties had no choice but to continue despite the struggles, differences, and no funding. It is safe to conclude that the law played a significant role in this partnership.

Partnerships take on many forms, and the leadership of each of the partners influences the type of interaction and collaboration. The role of universities in LSC training was influenced by the Chicago Public Schools leadership team. This new team instituted a funding process in which the universities took on the role of vendor. Previously, universities and nonprofit groups secured their own money, primarily from philanthropic foundations, to work with receptive schools. Dialogue and joint problem solving were now replaced by a more formal accountability system based on the bottom line. UIC was essentially given the role of a contractor, that is, UIC was responsible for the training; and the CPS administration often stated that because UIC was in charge, CPS did not have to "worry about it." Eventually, however, more collaboration occurred after UIC insisted that it could not work in isolation and a new CPS staff who valued collaboration took over. Even in very large organizations, the individual leaders involved seemed to make the most difference in defining the partnership.

Collaboration is not always beneficial on all accounts. Collaboration can result in the partners spending less time with those they are there to serve, for example, students, teachers, parents. In the TNT program, numerous meetings took place in which TNT staff and university and school personnel attempted to reach consensus about TNT's mission and goals. The contributions of UIC staff took time away from direct service delivery, for example, consulting with the teachers on teaching strategies. To gain the necessary trust, the focus was often on the process of collaboration rather than directly on the intended results (e.g., increased student learning, greater parental involvement).

In the TNT project, collaboration between UIC faculty and principals was based on the notion of each school being a unique TNT school. Principals acknowledged that TNT represented an intrusion into their work as leaders. It also took time to assimilate the extra staff and ideas into their local culture. They were reluctant to lose their span of control because they wanted TNT to be a part of *their* agenda, not the university's. The initial goal of a "win-win" situation took several years for some local school personnel to view as realistic and achievable. For others, the notion of a joint agenda never developed. Based on the evaluations and observations of the first two years, principals responded to the TNT initiatives in "generally cautious, strategic and conserving ways" (Smylie, Crowson, Chou, and Levin, 1994: 352). While not all behaved identically, they often compartmentalized the project, keeping it separate from the routine school functions. TNT was regarded as a set of resources to enhance their school, and thus principals wanted to establish various control mechanisms to influence TNT implementation (Smylie et al., 1994). The challenge became one of jointly setting the agenda, while not usurping the control of the principals. Specific programmatic features of TNT still exist in some of the schools but developing socially integrated service community schools still remains an over-riding goal; currently, the TNT model is not the salient and cohesive school culture in all of the schools.

In the LSC project, after some initial attempts to share the ad-ministrative part of training, the partners agreed that the CPS school should handle site selection, registration, and monitoring of the LSC members. If the autonomy of a partner is critical to achieving the goal, it is often more efficient and effective for others to trust that partner and get out of the way.

Assessment of social partnerships is challenging. Determining the success of collaboration was difficult in both initiatives. Since the LSC training activities had more discrete boundaries, success or fail-ure appeared more apparent on the surface. But the impact of such endeavors is often latent. A January 1996 letter to Lacelles Anderson, the principal investigator of The Nation of Tomorrow, seven years after its beginning, from Jack Mawbey of the W. K. Kellogg Founda-tion, illustrates this dilemma nicely:

> I have been continually impressed by the project generally,
> but this particular report [sixth year report] has made me even
> more aware of the uniqueness of each of the Chicago schools
> involved, their individual successes, barriers to progress, and
> challenges. Although many of those who made the project
> so successful will not be physically present, those who remain
> are more skilled, more knowledgeable, and more empowered
> to continue to improve their educational programs for the
> youngsters in their schools. In my way of thinking, that is true
> sustainability.

This statement illustrates the catalytic enduring impact of TNT from one perspective, but the evidence is soft, that is, it represents one person's opinion. Hard data such as changes in student achieve-ment are often available, but generalizations about connections let alone causal relationships between an intervention and an outcome must be made cautiously.

The politics of an evaluation also cannot be dismissed. Several audiences—public funding agencies, school administration, teach-ers, university faculty—all have a vested interest in the results. The publicness of the two projects ensured that they received consid-

erable attention and at times a critical eye. Funders and school officials wanted to know whether the TNT intervention was sustainable
given the large influx of external funds. CPS officials and reform
groups saw the success and failure of LSC training often in terms of
power—will good training enhance the authority of LSCs?

*Faculty scholarship emerges from social partnerships but also in-
fluences the collaborative work of the partners.* In the LSC project, university professors became more involved in writing the content of
the program as time progressed. What faculty members often lacked
in experiential knowledge and hands-on involvement with training
local citizens, they made up for in their experience of pedagogy and
knowledge of educational reform in general. They were better able
to think "out of the box" because they did not feel compelled to de-
fend past practices, were more intellectually self-confident (maybe
even arrogant at times), and more skilled at writing and interpreting
concepts and information into a theoretical context. Thus, the differ-
ing perspectives became reinforcing and complementary once mutual trust existed.

Just as the final product of LSC training was considered by the reformers and school personnel to be of better quality because of faculty engagement, so faculty scholarship also improved. Their involvement not only made their work more socially relevant, but their
engagement enhanced the quality of their scholarly work. For instance, they included examples from LSC training in their articles for
publication. Faculty members who were engaged in the TNT project
redefined their scholarship. For some, they not only wrote about
their engagement, but also altered the focus of their research agendas, putting more stress on the urban context and the problems of
student development.

*Continuous support for collaboration is required for long-term im-
pact.* Although TNT was a major campus outreach project, no formal administrative structure or long-term financial support of TNT
from UIC had been established at the time of implementation. The
primary funding came from the Kellogg Foundation with matching
funds from the offices of the University of Illinois President and UIC
Chancellor for the duration of the five-year period. Professor Larry
Nucci, one of the main architects, concluded: "TNT began without
up-front genuine institutional commitments. We have tried to operate a new institutional structure ostensibly as a faculty research proj-

ect. . . . This strategy actually makes a great deal of sense if you hope to run an institutional experiment without external interference, and without any long-term institutional obligations. It makes no sense at all however, as a basis for continued activity" (1994).

LSC training was based on an unfunded legislative mandate, although there was an implicit understanding that state funds newly allocated for Great Cities initiatives at UIC would be used for this project. Legislators also opined that corporate and foundation funds were quite accessible. Even though the law specifically stated that the CPS were not obligated to support LSC training, CPS did provide funds to cover printing and some administrative costs.

The lack of funds significantly altered the approach to training. Volunteer help became more important and the scope of the project had to be reduced. For example, the reform community initially argued very strongly that the participants' 200-page handbook be available in at least four languages (Chinese, English, Polish, and Spanish), but they settled for two (English and Spanish). UIC had to convince the reform community that no private funds were available and that UIC and other universities had limited or no funds earmarked for this venture. Several months elapsed before all parties generally accepted this position, but tension still existed about future funding and the ownership of the training, depending on its funding sources.

Leaders at UIC learned that long-term commitments are necessary for outreach endeavors. The UIC Neighborhoods Initiative, a program like TNT, has a ten-year commitment of UIC institutional support. This long-term support is based in part on the lessons UIC learned about the limited sustainability of TNT, once external support for TNT disappeared. In short, both long-term and short-term support for projects are required. A promise of stability and vitality is needed early on for initial commitment and sustaining power.

Summary

Faculty members who became involved in both collaborations quickly learned several lessons: that collaborative work often creates a conflict of institutional cultures; that political and community groups want to use the prestige of the university to advance their agenda; that faculty members often have less *experiential* knowledge of the problem context than do teachers and reformers but compensate by using their theoretical perspectives; that failed experiments outside the academy are more visible than a failed experiment in a laboratory; that compromise is essential; that new forms of communication are needed to reach different audiences; that partnerships can advance the university agenda; that partnerships can be intellectually exciting and challenging; that faculty scholarship is enhanced; and that continuous support is needed for long-term impact.

For many faculty members and administrators, the basic perspective on collaboration has changed from a view that the university can help provide solutions to social problems to one which suggests that the university is *jointly responsible* for reform in partnership with local schools, civic leaders, and parents. The obligation of the university under this social contract is to be an active voice for the community and for society. It was asked to become an advocate for social justice in our society. Thus issues of "what ought to happen" became more salient, issues that challenged the dominant intellectual culture at a research university.

These two projects, however, led to disillusionment among other members of faculty about the difficulty of the work, the lack of recognition from peers, the slow publication rate, the loss of control over research, the time away from campus, the threat of not getting tenure, and discouraging criticism from senior tenured faculty. This engagement thus brought vividly to reality the fundamental and unresolved issue of the appropriateness of this type of individual and collective faculty work in a research university. Faculty involvement produced some strong advocates and champions but some tired and burned-out people as well.

Implications for Higher Education

Our reflections on the Great Cities Initiatives and similar initiatives around the country convince us that the success of new partnerships between the community and the university will depend on substantial changes in higher education, particularly at research universities, not just adjustments to the campus reward system or similar forms of tinkering around the edges, but central shifts in institutional mission and focus. The changes must begin with the social contract between higher education and the greater community. The good news is that some of these changes are already under way (El-Khawas, 1996). We list several implications.

RENEGOTIATING THE SOCIAL COVENANT

In 1940 the American Association of University Professors (AAUP) and the Association of American Colleges (AAC) issued a joint "Statement of Principles on Academic Freedom and Tenure," a document that is still in force. Its first paragraph included this admonition: "Institutions of higher education are conducted for the *common good* and not to further the interest either of the individual teacher or the institution as a whole. The common good depends upon the free search for truth and its free exposition" (AAUP, 1995: 3).

What is the "common good"? The AAUP statement does not say explicitly, but it implies that as long as faculty work is driven by a search for truth and not by more venal motives, the common good will be served. As we have already noted, the public has become impatient with this—not necessarily because they reject the ideas of academic freedom as expressed by the AAUP, but because they see faculty work as increasingly selfish and privatized. They see academic freedom, in other words, as a smokescreen for furthering the interests of the individual faculty member and those of the institution. As Eugene Rice has observed, "Higher education is regarded by all too many as a private benefit, not a public good. Viewed in this light, the kinds of solid financial support higher education has enjoyed over the past half century, student aid, and even tenure, make little sense to the general public" (1996: 4).

If we accept the general notion that the common good is the expression of the interests of free people in a democratic society, negotiated in ways which have positive social consequences, then the nature of the academy's contribution to the common good becomes clearer. In the following pages we argue that the role of the modern university is not only to become more responsive to social problems but also to serve as a meeting place—actual or symbolic—for the expression and negotiation of social discourse. Both of these roles have significant implications for the nature of faculty work and the focus of academic leadership.

Becoming More Responsive

The general public is seeking greater engagement with social issues from the academy, demanding that higher education better prepare the young for work, frame research agendas in ways that address social ills, and do away with the traditional attitude of noblesse oblige toward community service. Land grant institutions, in particular, were formed to serve these values directly. Being useful to society was a primary reason for their existence. But during the past half-century the research university has become a more exclusive professional organization, with peer-reviewed research productivity dominating its culture. Knowledge, solely or primarily for its own sake, has become a primary justification for faculty investment. Research productivity, as defined by the number of peer-reviewed journal articles and books published, is often the criterion of success. Thus, the academy has turned inward for its character and sense of worth and being. Its separation from society has been conscious, deliberate, and defining.

And thus, the AAUP / AAC statement, while still largely valid today, needs a codicil: Academic freedom characterized by the "free search for truth and its free exposition" will serve the common good *as long as* communities beyond the academy are involved in defining the goals of the search and are active participants in it. Universities must continually look outward and not inward to remain vibrant and useful to society; otherwise, they will become victimized by their own myopia. This stance, of course, does not mean that basic research in education or in any discipline should play only a minor role in the academy (Getzels, 1978). Basic research challenges the conventional wisdom, provides theoretical understandings for complex phenomena, and encourages experimentation unfettered by a predetermined agenda.

Part of the difficulty in attempting to inject more social relevance into faculty scholarship is the perception that as relevance increases, academic rigor necessarily decreases. In fact, both are essential. When brave faculty members have ventured into collaborative efforts to understand and solve societal ills, they have often discovered that their claims on truth are rather fragile and incomplete. For example, in Chicago many of the most knowledgeable experts on school reform do not reside in the academy. Few would argue that university professors have all the answers to what works in school reform. Many faculty members would say that what works is a naive notion because what works in education depends upon so many interacting variables that are impossible to control. Peter Ewell, a contributor to this volume, has observed that research in higher education needs to leave behind questions like "What is the effect of X, all other things being equal?" and embrace questions like, "What is the impact of Program X on Group Y in setting Z?" (1996).

Political judgments, however, must be made, and the question for educators is whether they stand ready to make these judgments more informed. This means doing more than simply laying out the results of the research studies, however carefully designed they are; it means having the researchers take the extra step of working with those affected by the results to determine the meaning of those results and the implications for future policy.

We must also rid ourselves of the distinction between academic truth and political truth (Corry, 1994). For years, the university has assumed and communicated to the citizenry that universities possess a higher order of truth. Bender (1993) argues that universities can serve society better by following John Dewey's argument that they are participants in a community of truth makers always searching for but never finding ultimate truths.

As we slowly accept the idea of multiple realities, we begin to realize that not all of these lie within the exclusive domain of the university or of academic practice. But in doing so we need to be aware that making academic boundaries more permeable could introduce a sort of hopeless relativism, where no one perspective or argument is seen as more credible than any other.

Recent and more moderating responses in the academy are evident. One is how we classify and characterize faculty scholarship. Ernest Boyer's (1990) proposal to expand scholarship to include teaching, integration, and application, in addition to discovery, has created considerable faculty interest about the work of faculty. Public service—applied scholarship—is more salient today, a development which faculty in land-grant institutions should especially applaud. Mary Walshok, in her book *Knowledge Without Boundaries* (1995), elaborates on what universities can do for the economy, the workplace, and the community. Her message, in short, is that we can benefit from our analysis of the work of faculty if we accept the premise that faculty can be teachers as well as scholars and professional service providers as well as researchers.

Providing a Setting

The university can also redefine its commitment to the common good by becoming a setting for an expanded social discourse. While the academy rarely can solve important social problems, it can promote learning about how problems might be solved. While the academy cannot presume to have sole access to higher truths, it can play a major role in the search for them. While faculty members do not hold the secrets to the common good, they can be active participants in defining and shaping it. Seeking and holding truths need not be divorced from personal experiences and knowledge. And while the academy needs to provide more judgments of excellence and value to multiple audiences, it cannot fall into the trap of practicing judgmentalism (John Boyle, 1996).

IMPLICATIONS FOR FACULTY WORK

The heart of faculty work rests on influence: the impact on students, peers, professionals in one's field, and the general populace. The increasing fragmentation and privatization of faculty work has made such outlets for faculty talents more difficult to find. Russell Jacoby (1987), in his book *The Last Intellectuals*, complained that academic specialists, rather than sophisticated generalists, have come to dominate intellectual life. However, in the March 1995 issue of the *Atlantic Monthly*, Robert S. Boynton argued that a resurgence of public intellectual activity had recently occurred. Public intellectuals want to influence public policy. They do not wish to keep their ideologies solely within the academic community; instead, they wish to have a wider audience, to publish in journals, magazines, and media outlets that have a diverse and large audience. They are willing to express their ideas in nonacademic language and to use different formats for referencing ideas, arguing rationale, and presenting findings. Today, they reside at university campuses all over the country, and they are often female or Black academics shaped by the social activism of the 1960s. It is interesting to observe that William Wilson, a noted urban sociologist at the University of Chicago, recently accepted a position at Harvard because "he was finally lured by the prospect of joining a brain trust of African-American thinkers there who are emerging as a powerful political and social voice in the country" (*Chicago Tribune*, January 8, 1996: A1). He and his new colleagues deliberately wish to revamp social policy for the nation. Forming social partnerships has become part of the landscape for their scholarly work.

Thomas Bender, writing about universities and the city, argues that "the metropolitan academic ought not work so hard at keeping the city at bay: it is a source of energy, of wonderfully complex intellectual problems, and of nonacademic intellectuals who have much to offer. What is needed is not the old university expert model, but a newer approach that facilitates continuing two-way conversations between the various academic groupings on the campus and the appropriate constituencies in the metropolis" (1996: 13).

Redefining the Epistemology of Faculty Work

The core issue of the academy is how faculty members know and acquire knowledge and understanding. Today's epistemologies have become complex, diffuse, inclusive, controversial, and not considered equally valid and valuable by all academy members. New ways of knowing and understanding are now in vogue, for example, autobiographical research, social theory, feminist perspectives, liberation theology, and qualitative research. The thread connecting all these is the belief that truth is not to be separated from personal experience. Thus, to the extent that the emerging perspectives of scholarship are both more political and more relevant, they parallel, without necessarily paying homage to, social forces pushing for change.

Rice (1996) noted that "all the work on reconsidering scholarship—or as the disciplinary societies prefer, the professional, scholarly, and creative work of faculty—is in the deepest sense an epistemological challenge" (14). Schon (1995) argues that new forms of scholarship to reflect a "knowing-in-action" are needed to complement the more traditional established forms of knowing. The most common ways of knowing in the universities—those based on the assumptions that theory-based knowledge is a purer form of truth than practice-based knowledge, and that practice is an extension of theory—appear inadequate to understanding so many of the human and societal problems and issues. Schon calls for "a kind of action research with norms of its own" (27).

More and more faculty members, particularly the younger and untenured, also want to integrate their societal concerns and perspectives into both their personal and professional lives. They express concern over the social relevance of their work. They are asking different kinds of questions, questions that have moral, social, and political implications. To them, the social utility of their research—linking research with action and social causes—needs to stand out. For example, many of the education professors at UIC personally care about changing schools and spend as much time engaged in designing and implementing interventions as they do in evaluating them. For faculty members in land-grant institutions, this marriage of being socially useful and scholarly is not new. But historically the linkage has not been as controversial as it now is. Today, the topics of research and education more often relate to societal problems, which introduce human, social, ethical, and spiritual dimensions, as well as political and economic perspectives. And so, the social pressures for new and more complex partnerships with the university are becoming stronger at the very time that newer faculty members seem most poised to meet them (Braskamp, 1996a).

This convergence of faculty and societal interests poses two scholarly challenges, however. Since these proactive activities often support an ideological position, do faculty members need to be open to others about their advocacy? And how can this form of scholarship be credible to peers who do not engage in such activities or who do not define scholarship in similar ways?

Redefining the Organization and Quality of Faculty Work

The academy is also reexamining how the quality of the work of the faculty is judged and rewarded. Massy and Wilger (1995) state that while those in higher education view themselves as the guardians of quality, quality is best viewed in terms of fitness for use by the intended consumers, namely students, academic colleagues, and the surrounding community. Thus, impact and influence on various audiences become part of the equation of judging the contributions of faculty. This perspective promotes inclusivity, reflective thought, dialogue, and analysis, but does not restrict scholarship.

The organization of faculty work, that is, how colleges structure and support all the work of the faculty, is also critical. Recently, several universities have tackled the conceptual issue of outreach scholarship and the pragmatic issues related to the institutional support of faculty work. For example, the University of Minnesota (1993), Michigan State University (Votruba, 1996), and University of Illinois at Urbana–Champaign (Farmer and Schomberg, 1993) have attempted to explicitly classify outreach and engagement as a scholarly activity, using contributions to the public welfare or the common good as one criterion.

The language used to describe the work of outreach is critical. The very term *outreach* has a paternalistic connotation, implying that it is the civic duty of faculty to impart their wisdom to others. Similarly, the use of such terms as *technology and information transfer* imply one-way communication, an incomplete definition. The University of Minnesota's definition of outreach is more descriptive of the work: "Outreach is the transfer and exchange of knowledge between the institution and society" (1993: 1). Ernest Lynton, in his book *Making the Case for Public Service* (1995), provides an extensive argument for a dynamic interactive dialogue between various audiences, especially the practitioners. Mutual influence is fostered through dialogue, a point reinforced by the late Ernest Boyer (1996) in his argument for the scholarship of engagement.

IMPLICATIONS FOR ACADEMIC LEADERSHIP

Recommitting faculty work in the ways just described calls for a new form of academic leadership. What then should the new leadership's priorities be? We suggest six.

First, at the most basic level, academic leaders need to recognize what motivates faculty professionals: autonomy, control over one's own destiny, challenging work, a sense of efficacy, and a feeling of contributing to a larger good (Maehr and Braskamp, 1986). The historic problem for many is that autonomy and the larger good have been considered to be mutually exclusive values. We see no such incompatibility, however. Academic units can become genuine communities of interest, brought together by vigorous inquiry into broad, mutually-negotiated agendas and by the diverse strengths and interests of their members. Such an environment, in fact, is far more conductive to individual faculty autonomy than the one-set-of-criteria-must-fit-all kind of culture we see in most places today. In that sense common purpose can, ironically, reinforce academic freedom (Wergin, 1994).

Second, academic leaders need to support commonality as well as uniqueness. To do away with common standards is to do away with the common good. We should not confuse quality with conformity. Having standards does not mean standardization. Deans and department chairs must ensure that all forms of inquiry are advanced and defended provided they meet canons of excellence. The problem with some of the new forms of inquiry is that research and advocacy can become confused. Leaders can help by supporting truth *seeking* and questioning truth *holding*, which fosters smugness and self-absorption.

Third, academic leaders must publicly recommit the university to the common good, and in doing so they need to recognize this paradox: that the more relevant to the public good faculty work becomes, the more important academic freedom becomes. Universities cannot be for-profit consulting firms, the primary interventionist hired by another agency. Neither can they be "vendors of packaged education products" (Novak, 1992: 80). The motive is not profit but the common good, and faculty work must be described and communicated in those terms.

Academic leaders thus need new skills as reality shapers. They need to be able to sit beside their internal and external colleagues (faculty, students, citizens, politicians) in ways that persuade one and all to be clear about what higher education should and should not deliver. Institutions, per se, must not be advocates of social policy, but should instead foster individual faculty understandings and communications of social policy in a free and open environment.

By law and tradition the public university has been reluctant to take political or moral stands. The problem is that the academy itself is political. An underlying tenet of education is that it is a key way to enable individuals to increase their economic and cultural capital, and nothing is more political than that. And so the idea that universities should aspire to be apolitical institutions is naive. Then what should the academy's political agenda be? We agree with Robert Armour's suggestion (1995) that "the institution must do the *moral* thing, not the *political* one. Speaking out against injustice is a moral act, and if it has political implications they are not for the academic institution to act upon, but for the political ones to do so." External constituencies need to know that colleges and universities cannot become toadies to shifting political agendas. Academic institutions have an obligation to society to encourage as well as protect the intellectual and academic freedom of the faculty. Perhaps a major criticism of faculty members is that they *underuse* the privileges of tenure for society's benefit.

Through partnerships, the research and instructional agenda can be intricately connected to the communities outside the academy. We need to be clear about our assets—our strengths, our unique contributions and roles. The university must also consider its legitimate long-term self-interest and its fundamental mission when negotiating its partnership with society. For example, in the LSC training, we quickly learned we had to focus on the education and training of LSC members and not on the politics of LSCs in school governance.

Fourth, faculty members must be involved in the partnerships. Participants in the social partnerships should not consist only of temporary staff and faculty members not eligible for tenure. If the work of partnerships is an institutional priority, the core of the staff, tenured faculty, must provide the leadership and become engaged. Only teaching and research faculty can integrate all the work of the university around the theme of scholarship.

The funding of partnerships must be considered as well because it may uncover a dilemma about faculty motivation. Often partnerships are brought about through the advocacy of a champion, an individual faculty member with a cause. When partnerships are not brought about this way, administrators have a difficult time keeping faculty engaged, especially when the work becomes messy, political, and perceived as compromising to the ideals, norms, and reward structure of the academy (McPherson, 1992). For example, in both the TNT and LSC projects, individual professors conveniently withdrew when given an opportunity to do so. Partners rather than individual entrepreneurs need to be rewarded, and collaborative endeavors and appropriate infrastructures are needed. Since external funders often are not in the habit of funding organizational structures, but instead fund direct services to the communities in which universities are a partner, long-term institutional support from the leadership is essential.

Fifth, leaders need to assess faculty work more completely. Expectations of and for faculty members must become a greater part of the dialogue that chairs and deans have with all constituencies, but especially the faculty. The Latin root of *assessment* is *assidere*, "to sit beside." This term brings to mind images like these: engagement, involvement, interaction, trust; caring, reflection, collaboration; coaching, sharing, consultation; community. *Sitting beside* implies dialogue and discourse, understanding the other's perspective before making value judgments. Good assessment is a developmental process, always incorporating accountability, autonomy, and assistance in the equation. To sit beside is to recognize unique talents and skills, and to recognize each professor as a valuable member of a community (Braskamp and Ory, 1994: 12). Thus faculty can be judged for both their merit—"quality according to the standards of the profession"—and their worth—"benefit to the institution, the meeting of needs" (Scriven, in Braskamp, 1996b).

Faculty engagement in larger societal issues will force universities to be more explicit about faculty expectations at the time of hiring as well as throughout their careers. Linking society and institutions of higher education is useful in another important way. It allows for external validation of the work of the faculty. For individual faculty members and programs, "standing within the university comes from standing without the university" (Murphy, 1996).

Sixth and finally, academic leaders need to address more publicly the issue of the "specialness" of the academy. No longer does society allow us to enjoy this uniqueness unconditionally. In an issue of *Change* magazine, Clark Kerr, former president of the University of California, concluded, "Universities enjoyed their autonomy historically as a result of their ethical conduct, and now, for the first time in American history, it may be said that they could be in the process of losing some of it for the same reason" (1994: 15). If the academy loses its specialness, it will reduce some of its value to society. Thus, leaders and academy members need to recognize this paradox of simultaneously holding on to faculty autonomy and serving the common good through social partnerships. As faculty members become more involved in public service, this tension only becomes more noticeable. These engaged academics need more than ever to begin a dialogue with others about how they individually and collectively can best fulfill a special role in society.

When universities become engaged in such goals as urban revitalization, the universities themselves can become socially transformed. This was part of the intent of the Kellogg Foundation when it funded TNT. It is this linkage that challenges faculty values and knowledge—the uncomfortable insight, for example, that an accumulated wisdom exists beyond the campus which faculty may not even be aware of, much less privy to (Harkavy and Wiewel, 1995). Among the issues highlighted in this chapter, that of cultural diversity has emerged as a challenge that cannot be pushed aside or dealt with in abstract, postmodern terms. Intellectual elitism and a retreat to comfortable campus confines are not viable solutions.

In our view, the AAUP/AAC statement that worked so well as a galvanizing principle of academic freedom for more than a half century has no less currency today. But we delude ourselves if we think that this classic definition of the common good gives license to business as usual. The "free search for truth and its free exposition" must occur within an academic community where freedom *with* responsibility, not freedom *from* responsibility, is practiced. Higher education is not a sanctuary anymore. It is losing its insularity, having more claimants and partners now. The challenge is for higher education to be a very active partner in shaping its social relationship with society, being responsive while retaining its core purposes and standards.

References

American Association of University Professors (1995). *AAUP Policy Documents and Reports*, 8th ed. Washington, D.C.: AAUP.

Armour, R. (1995). Personal communication to Jon Wergin. May.

Bender, T. (1993). *Intellect and Public Life: Essays on the Social History of Academic Intellectuals in the United States*. Baltimore: Johns Hopkins University Press.

———. (1996). "Universities and the City: Scholarship, Local Life, and the Necessity of Worldliness." Keynote address at the International Conference, Amsterdam Centre for the Metropolitan Environment, University of Amsterdam, Amsterdam. March.

Boyer, E. L. (1990). *Scholarship Reconsidered: Priorities of the Professoriate*. Princeton, N.J.: Carnegie Foundation for the Advancement of Teaching.

———. (1996). "The Scholarship of Engagement." *Journal of Public Service and Outreach* 1(1), 11–20.

Boynton, R. S. (1995). "The New Intellectuals." *Atlantic Monthly*, 1(3), 53–70. March.

Boyle, J. (1996). Personal communication to Larry Braskamp. June.

Braskamp, L. A. (1996a). "Connections, Connectedness, and Central College." Presentation at Heritage Day, Central College, Pella, Iowa. May 31.

———. (1996b). "Evaluation of Faculty." *Dean's Dispatch, No. 84*. Chicago: College of Education, University of Illinois at Chicago.

Braskamp, L. A., and H. B. McPherson. (1995). Letter to Honorable Mary Lou Cowlishaw, House of Representatives, State of Illinois. May.

Braskamp, L. A., and J. C. Ory. (1994). *Assessing Faculty Work: Enhancing Individual and Institutional Performance*. San Francisco: Jossey-Bass.

Chicago Tribune. 8 January 1996. "U. of C. Is Losing Its Top Urban Sociologist." A1.

Corry, J. (1994). *Sifting and Winnowing Accountability/Assessment and Academic Freedom*. Madison: University of Wisconsin-Madison.

El-Khawas, E. (1996). *Campus Trends*. Washington, D.C.: American Council on Education.

Ewell, P. (1996). Personal communication to Jon Wergin. June.

Farmer, J. A., and S. F. Schomberg. (1993). *Faculty Guide for Relating Public Service to the Promotion and Tenure Review Process*. Champaign, Ill.: University of Illinois at Urbana-Champaign, Office of Continuing Education and Public Service.

Getzels, J. W. (1978). "Paradigm and Practice: On the Impact of Basic Research in Education." In *Impact of Research on Education: Some Case Studies*, ed. P. Suppes. Washington, D.C.: National Academy of Education.

Harkavy, I., and W. Wiewel. (1995). "Overview: University-Community Partnerships: Current State and Future Issues." *Metropolitan University*, 6(3), 7–14.

Hess, A. G., Jr. 29 November 1995. "Chicago's New Perspective on District Management." *Education Week*, 28.

Imig, D. (1996). *External Environment Scan: A Review of U.S. Trends as a Context for Teacher Education Policy*. Washington, D.C.: American Association of Colleges for Teacher Education. February.

Jacobs, D. (1996). "Kellogg Dean keeps School on Cutting Edge of Learning." *Chicago Sun-Times*, 3. January 21.

Jacoby, R. (1987). *The Last Intellectuals*. New York: Basic Books.

Kerr, C. (1994). "Knowledge, Ethics and the New Academic Culture." *Change*, 26(1), 8–15. January/February.

Klonsky, S. (1996). "'Da Mayor' Takes Over 'Da Schools'." *City Schools*, 1(1), 6–10.

Levin, R., ed. (1994). *Greater than the Sum: Professionals in a Comprehensive Services Model*. Washington D.C.: ERIC Clearinghouse on Teacher Education.

Lynton, E. A. (1995). *Making the Case for Professional Service*. Washington, D.C.: American Association for Higher Education.

Maehr, M. L., and L. A. Braskamp. (1986). *The Motivation Factor: A Theory of Personal Investment*. Lexington, Mass.: Lexington Books.

Massy, W. F., and A. K. Wilger. (1995). "Improving Productivity: What Faculty Think About It—and its Effect on Quality." *Change*, 27(4), 10–20. July/August.

McPherson, R. B. (1992). *Outreach in the College of Education: Reflections and Suggestions*. Chicago: College of Education, University of Illinois at Chicago.

Murphy, M. B. (1996). Personal communication to Larry Braskamp. June 22.

Novak, J. C. (1992). "Active Learning in Continuing Professional Education: The Challenge of Leadership." In *New Directions for Adult and Continuing Education, No. 56*, ed. P. J. Edelson, 63–81. Winter.

Nucci, L. (1994). Personal communication to Larry Braskamp. July.

Pick, G. (1995). "Nobel Laureate, University of Illinois President behind LSC Training Law." *Catalyst*, 29–30.

Putnam, R. D. (1995). "Bowling Alone: America's Declining Social Capital." *Journal of Democracy*, 6(1), 65–78. January.

Rice, E. (1996). *Making a Place for the New American Scholar*. Washington, D.C.: American Association of Higher Education.

Schon, D. A. (1995). "The New Scholarship Requires a New Epistemology." *Change*, 27(6), 27–34. November / December.

Smylie, M. A., R. Crowson, and V. Chou. (1994). "The Principal and Community— School Connections in Chicago's Radical Reform." *Educational Administration Quarterly*, 30(3), 342–64.

Stukel, J. (1994). *The State of the University of Illinois at Chicago*. Chicago: University of Illinois.

University of Minnesota (1993). *A Strategic Plan for Outreach*. Minneapolis: Office of the President.

Votruba, J. C. (1996). "Strengthening the University's Alignment With Society: Challenges and Strategies." *Journal of Public Service and Outreach*, 1(1), 29–36.

Walshok, M. L. (1996). *Knowledge Without Boundaries: What America's Research Universities Can Do for the Economy, the Workplace, and the Community*. San Francisco: Jossey-Bass.

Wergin, J. F. (1994). *The Collaborative Department: How Five Campuses are Inching toward Cultures of Collective Responsibility*. Washington, D.C.: American Association for Higher Education.

4

The Implications of the Changed Environment for Governance in Higher Education

ROGER BENJAMIN AND STEVE CARROLL

🎓 🎓 🎓

FOR WELL OVER A CENTURY, THE U.S. HIGHER EDUCATION SYSTEM HAS SET standards for equity and access for all citizens and excellence in academic achievement. There are ominous signs, however, that higher education is no longer able to respond to new challenges as vigorously and effectively as in the past. Fiscal problems now confront public and private institutions across the entire country. The resulting budget reductions threaten to plunge the sector into confusion and chaos. Moreover, there are growing concerns for low- and middle-income students' access to higher education, the extent to which the sector is meeting the needs of minority students, the quality of undergraduate education, the sector's contribution to the competitiveness of the American economy, and leadership turnover.

We argue that many of these concerns, though important in their own right, are symptoms or effects of a fundamental disjunction between higher education's changing environment and its governance system—the constellation of written and unwritten policies, procedures, and decision-making units that controls resource allocation within and among higher education institutions at all levels.[1]

As our collaborators have noted, the challenge to higher education emanates from dramatic changes simultaneously occurring in its role in society, the demographic composition of the student body, societal demands for research and service, the costs of instruction and research, and the availability of public support. Any one of these changes by itself would present significant new challenges to the system. However, the combination of changes now under way adds up to a threshold transformation of higher education's environment.

To respond to these changes effectively, higher education institutions and systems must be able to reallocate limited resources among competing demands. Unfortunately, higher education does not have a good track record in this area; examples of gross misallocations of resources are common. While some of these examples can be traced to poor or inattentive management, most stem from a deeper, more fundamental problem: the existing governance system in higher education cannot effectively cope with the problem of reallocating resources.

This places the policy focus squarely on governance. A redesigned governance system is a prerequisite for responding effectively to the various problems threatening higher education. In fact, the long-term question of whether higher education's governance system needs to be restructured is largely moot. Higher education's institutions and systems across the country are being *forced* to restructure themselves. And the numbers of institutions and systems forced to address the problems of identifying priorities, focusing on central missions, and reallocating resources are likely to grow. The central question is not whether but how higher education's governance system should be restructured.

This chapter offers our diagnosis of the problems that now confront higher education, our analysis of the problems, and policy guidelines that follow from the thesis that governance systems need restructuring. Notes on requirements for constructing an information and resource system are presented in an appendix. The information now available is not sufficient to conclusively demonstrate the validity of our thesis. However, higher education's leaders are now confronted with difficult problems that must be addressed in the near term. We offer this analysis in the hope that our observations will be helpful to those whose problems cannot be deferred until more complete information is available.

The Challenge of the Changed Environment

Recent economic, demographic, political, and social changes in U.S. society have dramatically come together to alter both the purposes higher education is asked to serve and the resources available to it.[2] Higher education is now faced with a new set of social roles and responsibilities, an increasingly diverse student population, new and changing demands from both students and society, limited or declining resources, and escalating costs. Together, these changes comprise a fundamentally new set of challenges to the higher education system.

THE ROLE OF THE SECTOR

For two centuries following the founding of Harvard in 1636, the American higher education system was comprised of small private colleges that focused on meeting the needs of an agrarian society. For the most part, they provided a *classical* education to a small number of citizens, primarily the sons of the wealthy. Society looked to the higher education system to provide professionals—ministers, doctors, and lawyers—and the political and social leadership to guide a new nation.

In 1826, Thomas Jefferson initiated a redefinition of the role of U.S. higher education. Jefferson saw mass public education as a way to cultivate the educated citizenry needed for economic development and democracy. His bold argument placed the future of the country squarely in the hands of a system that provided practical *technical* education at low cost to a sizable fraction of the population. The institutional inspiration, the land-grant university, was founded on the principles of access and excellence—access for all qualified applicants combined with the opportunity to achieve to one's fullest intellectual capacity.

Although the principles of access and excellence remain in place, today's postsecondary education system is expected to prepare the next generation of Americans to live in a postindustrial, information-centered global economy. Human capital is clearly becoming the central engine for economic growth and higher education is increasingly perceived as America's principal point of comparative advantage against international competitors.

CHANGING STUDENT DEMOGRAPHICS

Fueled by a combination of rapid growth in the traditional college-aged population and dramatic increases in participation by other groups, enrollments in colleges and universities grew rapidly from the turn of the century until World War II, then soared through the 1960s and into the early 1970s. The annual average rate of growth in higher education's enrollments exceeded 5 percent during the first sixty years of this century and increased to nearly 8 percent between 1960 and 1975. The rate of growth in enrollments then flattened dramatically, averaging between 1 and 2 percent through the late 1970s and the 1980s. However, as Figure 4.1 shows, the demand for enrollment will continue to grow into the next century, which means the pressure for resources to support the increased demand will also be likely to continue to increase.

While detailed data on students' characteristics are not available prior to 1965, the changes since then have been dramatic. The proportion of students who are female, older than the traditionally eighteen to twenty-one year olds, minority, or part time has grown considerably, both absolutely and relative to the proportion of their respective male, younger, white, or full-time counterparts. This growth in traditionally underrepresented populations is simultaneously one of the most impressive achievements and most difficult challenges of the higher education sector. Diversity has invigorated many campuses, and higher education is increasingly available to those who would once have been denied access. However, increased diversity presents new demands on higher education because of changing student needs, values, and aspirations. Some of these changes stem from the students' increasing need to balance school, work, and family obligations. Some stem from increasing numbers of underprepared students entering higher education. Others reflect fundamental challenges to the nature and substance of intellectual

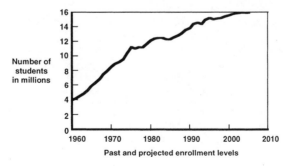

Figure 4.1. Demand for Enrollment Will Continue to Grow

inquiry. But, regardless of the source of these changes, traditional ways of doing business are proving increasingly inadequate.

DEMANDS FOR RESEARCH AND SERVICE

The changes in demands for research and services provided by higher education are striking, as well. Societal demands for basic research continue unabated. At the same time, higher education is increasingly expected to address the social issues of the day—everything from the causes of urban riots in Los Angeles to the need for a vaccine for AIDS. While universities are expected to continue research on field theory in physics, they are now also expected to make breakthroughs in applied fields, participate in university/industry partnerships, and even support start-up companies. And, as Braskamp and Wergin noted, society increasingly looks to higher education's institutions to directly stimulate local or state economic growth.

The pattern is similar with respect to demands for services. Familiar services such as agricultural extension and continuing education remain important ingredients in the service mix of many institutions. There also continues to be a steady increase in the number and type of miscellaneous services higher education institutions are expected to provide their communities. For example, universities are hosts for radio stations, elder hostels, airports, a variety of cultural centers, and real estate services. The list is very long. Finally, universities are increasingly expected to provide pro bono consulting and technical service to all levels of government.

FINANCES

Higher education was awash in new public money through the three decades following World War II. While the number of students to be served grew rapidly, the revenues governments made available for that purpose grew even faster, even after adjusting for inflation. With substantial increases in real public resources, colleges and universities could readily accommodate to the changing demands of growth without recourse to increased tuition and fees.

This picture changed dramatically in the late 1970s. Figure 4.2 indicates that since 1975 public support has not kept pace with the new demands on the higher education system. Specifically, financial support rose more slowly than enrollment demands from 1975 until 1990 and recently began to decline.

The rate of growth in the real resources governments provided to higher education fell sharply, averaging 1.8 percent from 1975 to 1990. Appropriations to higher education institutions declined in the first four years of this decade. Both state governments and the federal government are cutting support of higher education. Through tuition, students are making up some of the difference (see Figure 4.3). The question is, how long can this continue?

Finally, concurrent with this slowdown in the level of resources committed to higher education is the appearance of significant evidence that the costs of providing higher education are far outstripping inflation. For example, faculty salaries, a major component of higher education's costs, did not keep pace with inflation in the 1965–79 period. They have grown at an average annual rate that exceeded the rate of inflation since then.[3]

Other higher education costs grew more rapidly than inflation in the 1970s and 1980s as well. The costs of journals and books have grown at or above inflation rates over the past fifteen years. And many well-established higher education institutions began to face serious physical plant repair and maintenance issues in the 1980s, the result of decades of neglect and accounting practices that did not provide for physical capital depreciation.

Estimates of higher education's likely future revenues from governmental sources are not now available, but there is no reason to expect a turnaround anytime soon.[4] Thus, it appears that higher education is going to experience a lengthy period of slow growth, if not outright decline, in real public revenues per student.

Society continues to expect higher education to respond to traditional demands for instruction, research, and service but expects the postsecondary system to meet a wide variety of new demands as well. Its resources, however, are not growing as fast as are the demands it is expected to meet. If anything, the purchasing power of the resources available to higher education per student is declining.

Before the mid-1970s, the issue of where to cut expenditures rarely arose in higher education. Rather, the dominant problem was which of many new activities would be initiated this year and which would have to be deferred to a future date. The mid-1970s slowdown in revenue growth introduced an entirely new era. The combination of growing enrollments and minute increases in real revenues per student has meant that there is now very little annual growth in the

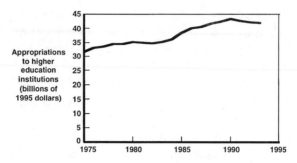

Figure 4.2. Public Support Has Not Kept Pace

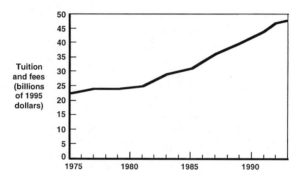

Figure 4.3. Students Are Making Up Some of the Difference

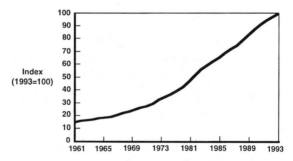

Figure 4.4. Costs in Higher Education are Growing Rapidly

real resources available to the sector. There is little new money. In this environment, these new activities can be supported only by cutting support for preexisting activities. Thus, the problem facing higher education decision makers is whether, not when, a new demand should be met, and, if so, which current activities should be cut back or terminated to accommodate the new activity.

To be sure, higher education institutions are not passive recipients of environmental forces. They may strive to modify or influence public perceptions and expectations of higher education. They can also attempt to increase the resources available to them. Although such efforts might ease pressures on the system for a time, they do not address the fundamental problem of allocating limited resources among competing demands. The demands on the system reflect social needs. Reducing demands on higher education implies that important social needs go unmet. Tuition and fee increases similarly substitute one problem—access—for another—revenue shortfalls. Higher education may be able to increase its revenues by offering new services. But the resources that must be devoted to the provision of new services will consume much of whatever new revenues are thereby generated, still leaving the problem of how to best allocate preexisting revenues among preexisting demands.

Higher education institutions and systems can also attempt to make better use of their resources through increased efficiency. Institutions have increased class sizes or asked faculty to teach extra courses. Yet asking faculty and staff to do more with less has obvious limits, as well as negative effects on the quality of instruction and research. The systems and institutions may generate cost savings through freezes on hiring, equipment purchases, travel, work furloughs, or incentives for early retirement. These and other methods may cut costs in the short run, but the results may leave critical functions unfulfilled, impose heavy burdens on some staff and faculty, and limit the ability of the institution to pursue quality or excellence. Furthermore, unless those costs which are cut are for entirely unnecessary activities, quality must eventually suffer.

In any event, regardless of the institutions' and systems' success in reducing expectations, attracting increased revenues, and improving efficiency, higher education is now faced with new and changing demands from both students and society, in circumstances of limited or even declining resources, and escalating costs. To respond effectively to changing demands, higher education institutions and systems must be able to reallocate their limited resources. The primary management challenge facing higher education leaders is to allocate the available resources in ways that best meet the demands placed on their institutions.

Resource Allocation in Higher Education

The current governance system evolved in an environment of rapid, sustained growth. Budgets grew as fast as did enrollments. Any changes in students' demands could be accommodated by increases in overall budgets; there was little need to think of reallocating resources from existing programs to new ones. Most higher education institutions and systems evolved decentralized and stovepiped governance structures in which organizational entities or components such as departments, which may themselves employ participatory decision-making principles, report to higher-level organizations, with little communication between entities at the same level. The specifics differ across higher education institutions and systems. Context, history, tradition, size, complexity, and mission are all important considerations. However, irrespective of the many differences among institutions and systems, the common principles, routines, and practices of the governance structures found in most higher education institutions and systems constrain reallocation of resources and, in so doing, limit higher education's ability to adjust to a changed environment.

The governance system that emerged to deal with the problem of growth is highly decentralized in that individual units and departments have a great deal of autonomy over how they allocate their resources. In the typical institution or system, the various academic and administrative units operate independently and in isolation from one another. Within a single university, for example, the dean of the College of Arts and Sciences may allocate resources among the several dozen social science, humanities, life science, and physical science departments; the dean of engineering may do the same for a variety of engineering programs; and the vice president for operations may do the same for departments such as facilities maintenance, parking, and campus security. Yet these processes occur largely in isolation from one another. Furthermore, each academic department has considerable independence in making decisions about how to use their allocation. Departments generally make major decisions regarding goals, curricula, and new hires internally, with subsequent review and refinement by the academic administration and Faculty Senate.

Yet, the governance system is hierarchical in the sense that departmental chairs report to deans, who in turn report to vice presidents. The collegiate or administrative units report up or down but tend not to be connected horizontally to collateral collegiate or administrative units. At the system and state level the salient characteristics of the governance system are similar. The central administrators of the community college system report to a state postsecondary authority but typically have little or no relationship with the state college or university systems within their states. The university system leaders similarly have little or no knowledge of the state college or community college systems.

Even those leaders at the very top of the governance hierarchy, however, must build coalitions with administrative and faculty leaders in order to implement change successfully. Higher education governance is largely consensual, and few presidents or chancellors can impose their will without the support of the faculty senate and other key decision-making groups. Consensual decision making generally acts as a conservative force, slowing the rate of change, avoiding extremes, and protecting the pursuit of multiple goals and objectives.

Another salient characteristic of higher education governance is its complexity, particularly within large research universities. For example, UCLA's College of Letters and Science includes 36 academic departments, 25 interdepartmental degree programs, 10 organized research units, 4 focused research units, 5 centers, and 12 other freestanding organizations. Although this college is complex itself, it is only one of the university's thirteen schools and colleges. Additionally, the institution includes over 72 support units concerned with activities ranging from parking to student counseling.[5] Outside the institution, accrediting agencies, the state legislature, and a variety of special interest and advocacy groups exert pressure and sometimes require the college to respond to demands ranging from the content and rigor of the curriculum to the number of books in the library. It is difficult to imagine how to manage this structure effectively.

Limitations of the Current Governance System

The current governance system presents severe challenges to the administrators of any college or university confronted with changing demands and limited resources. For example, the current financial climate forces administrators to consider trade-offs such as whether the institution should hire an assistant professor of economics, provide resources for research equipment for a physics institute, or fund more student counselors. However, communication and information typically flows along narrow vertical columns, with few feedback loops or horizontal linkages. Negotiation about allocation decisions is two-way, with messages going up to the dean or down to the department. The complexity and weak horizontal linkages inhibit comparative analyses to assess the relative merits of the competing proposals. And the influence of various stakeholder and constituent groups may reduce the real options open to administrators.

Economists, for example, may be able to argue persuasively the necessity for econometrics, given the presence of an economics department. They may able to point to minimum critical mass required for an economics department to cover the agreed upon core undergraduate and graduate curriculum of economics—agreed upon by economists. Economists are also considered the best judges of fellow economists' published research and are therefore best suited to deciding who to hire and recommend for tenure and promotion. But economists have little experience, standing, or competence concerning the relative merits of additional expenditures for physics research equipment or student counselors. In other words, economists can make the case for their unit, but do not have the decision-making evaluation criteria or information useful in evaluating the case for the physics institute or, more importantly, comparing the cases of the two units.

When faced with the necessity to go beyond the across-the-board cuts strategy that is possible under the current governance system, a department-based, bottom-up approach is not feasible. Indeed, university administrators often reach this conclusion, which typically leads to the error most frequently committed when higher education institutions are faced with the necessity of choice: the top-down strategy.

When faced with the necessity of choice, the only decision makers with formal authority and relevant information are deans or central administrators. Indeed, under immediate threat of fiscal cutbacks, central administrators do propose sweeping cuts of entire departments, professional schools, collegiate units, or even branch campuses. Such attempts virtually always fail to be carried out, and they fail for the same reasons department-based solutions are doomed—absence of comparative information and decision-making evaluation criteria. Because central administrators have been used to operating in vertical relationships with academic units under their authority, they also lack the means to compare the costs and benefits of hiring an economist versus acquiring physics research equipment.

Academic units argue that they are unique; only economists can judge the qualifications of economists. Thus academic units targeted for cuts invariably can and do make a strong case for the preservation or enhancement of their program based on absolute criteria; for example, the department of speech communication is important to the goals of research, teaching, and service and, moreover, this particular department of speech communication needs additional funding to increase its quality.

The academic units selected out by central administrators for fiscal cuts or elimination also argue that they were not given an opportunity to present their case, based on their data and their criteria. This usually is a strong argument, because appropriate statistical information concerning the cost of the academic program, faculty / student ratios, and output measures are seldom collected routinely by central administrators. Moreover, because central administrators have targeted particular academic units for cuts, those units then can argue that potential alternative cuts of other units have not been adequately explored—they have been unfairly singled out.

The top-down solution is therefore usually rejected by the faculty that make up the academic units. The faculty, many of whom have tenure, successfully argue that the top-down strategy and recommendations are illegitimate, that they violate the collegial decentralized nature of the governance structure in place. Indeed, there are significant numbers of higher education institutions that have been damaged by top-down efforts which were eventually aborted, but which nonetheless left individual academic units weakened because of negative publicity, the sense of collegiality between departments and central administrators destroyed, and the reputation of the institution tarnished. Attempts at setting priorities defining missions and making choices that fail to be implemented can create more problems for the institution than it faced before it began the process.

New Governance Systems: Guidelines for Change

The current governance structure is unable to support decision makers in setting priorities and differentiating missions, nor does it compel or even encourage implementation of any priorities or choices made. Because of this, or perhaps as a function of it, the current governance system does not have in place comparative, university-wide evaluation criteria for decision making. When faced with the necessity to reduce budgets in academic units, most higher education institutions typically prefer the strategy of mandating across-the-board fiscal cuts. This strategy is seen as fair because everyone shares the pain equally. However, if the fiscal cuts continue long enough and are deep enough, the negative effects of this strategy become clear. If fiscal stringency persists, responsible faculty members and administrators must begin to weigh alternative strategies. This imperative translates into the need for a governance system that sets priorities, focuses missions, and compels or facilitates implementation of choices made.

THE CONTEXT

The current decentralized, incremental governance structure exists in a supportive decision-making culture typically shared by faculty if not administrators and staff. Effective innovations must be sensitive to the context—the local environment and culture. The history of educational reform repeatedly demonstrates the futility of imposing externally developed solutions on an institution or system. It is important to recognize that the only appropriate groups to develop and implement improved governance structures are the constituencies within the existing governance structures of higher education institutions and postsecondary systems.

Because there is little or no experience in reallocation, there is likely to be considerable reluctance on the part of all parties, but especially faculty, to allow the decentralized governance system and the culture that supports it to be transformed. Under conditions of financial stress, for example, participants—faculty, staff, students, and interest groups—will question even the most basic and apparently neutral information and analyses. Without a sense of how a new governance structure would improve on the present one, faculty are unlikely to abandon the old structure even with all its present flaws.

However, when retrenchment makes reallocation inevitable, this gives all participants in the current governance system strong incentives to search for a better way to carry out retrenchments in a less damaging fashion.

SETTING PRIORITIES

Because past eras of incremental growth enabled higher education to pursue multiple goals simultaneously, it did not need to develop ways to clarify priorities. In the face of retrenchment, however, institutions face new pressure to cut the areas of lowest priority while maintaining the areas of highest priority. Given the absence of any consensus among decision makers about what these high and low priority areas are, some criteria are needed to establish priorities.

To go beyond the current governance structure requires evaluation criteria that permit comparison, for example, of physics versus economics. However, the development of such comparative evaluation criteria also requires wide discussion in order to generate an agreed-upon set of definitions and contexts to which they should apply. The criteria need to reflect the input of diverse units and individuals because they are ultimately a reflection of organizational values.

Although it would appear difficult, if not impossible, to develop comparative decision-making evaluation criteria, in our experience such criteria are explicitly developed whenever higher education institutions are forced to go beyond across-the-board cuts in their budgets. Then, just as in any other public or private institution, appropriate decision makers, assisted by committees, develop criteria that can be the basis for comparative evaluation of seemingly unlike academic and nonacademic functions. The following criteria were developed by one of the authors (Roger Benjamin) from actual practice and are offered as an illustration of what might be more routinely developed and implemented: [6]

1. Quality. This applies to the quality of the faculty (in teaching, research, and service), the students, library collections, and services provided. Both locally designed and standardized quality measures can be used. Indicators of quality include faculty publications, patents, and citations; national ratings and rankings; attrition or graduation rates; and results of standardized assessments. In our experience, departments, centers, institutes, schools, or colleges can be ranked in three to five categories ranging from nationally recognized units to units of poor, problematic quality.

2. Centrality. Each program should be evaluated in terms of its contribution to the mission of the institution, or system. For example, participants could determine the degree to which the program is an essential component of a liberal arts, preprofessional, or professional education that is regarded as central to the institution's or system's mission. Every academic department may claim it is central to carrying out the university's mission. However, while it may be difficult to imagine an arts and sciences college without an English department, it may well be possible to imagine the elimination of a weak unit of the social sciences or languages which would still leave in place representatives of the mode or style of inquiry. The typical institutional mission statement that emphasizes teaching, research, and service may be too broad to provide meaningful guidance in this task. Thus consideration of other written documents (e.g., strategic plans or accreditation self-studies) as well as discussion among policy makers and practitioners is required.

3. Demand and Workload. Both short-term and long-term demands for each program (increasing, stable, or declining) must be considered in priority-setting. Demand indicators might include trends in the number of applications, admissions, and take rates as well as trends in students' choice of majors; services performed in support of other programs; instruction of students or research for the solution of pressing societal problems; and the prospective market for graduates. Most institutions calculate and track faculty workload (based very generally on the number of courses offered or students enrolled in courses).

4. Cost Effectiveness. Because aspirations are always limited by the resources available, programs must be continually examined to see if more economical or efficient ways are possible to accomplish the same ends. Yet cost alone must not govern the decision; the effectiveness of the program must also be weighed. When taken together, cost and effectiveness provide one important measure of whether funds are being put to the best use.

5. Comparative Advantage. What is the rationale for the program at the institution or system? What are the unique characteristics of each program that make it essential to the community, region, nation or other programs within the institution or system? For example, in order to apply the concept of comparative advantage, the place of the higher education institution in the ecology of the regional or state higher education system should be considered. If institution A's engineering college is of poor quality but institution B's engineering college, in the same metropolitan area, is of high quality, perhaps the leaders of institution A should reallocate their resources to an academic program of greater quality. In addition, the rationale for a Scandinavian area studies program may be high in Wisconsin or Minnesota, where many citizens of Scandinavian descent reside, but low in, say, Southern California, where a large Latino population suggests an area studies program devoted to Latino interests.

OBTAINING COMPARATIVE INFORMATION

Following the establishment of agreed-upon criteria for establishing priorities, the next step is to assess various departments, divisions, or institutions against the criteria. This process requires standardized, comparative information about each unit. Ideally, multiple measures will be used for each criterion in order to broaden the range of information and increase the validity of overall ratings. The usefulness of comparative information for decision making also requires that the information is publicly available and perceived as accurate and meaningful.

Both quantitative and qualitative data may contribute to the development of this information base. For example, departmental rankings provide quantitative (ordinal) measures of quality, and the ratio of student to faculty FTEs provides a quantitative (interval) measure of workload. On the other hand, centrality or comparative advantage are perhaps best assessed through interviews with preeminent faculty (both internal and external to the unit under review), essays prepared by department chairs, or academic program reviews.[7]

The development of criteria for decision making, coupled with information about the extent to which diverse units meet these criteria, greatly enlarges organizational capacity for resource reallocation. When faced with the necessity to make difficult choices, decision makers have some analytic tools at their disposal. This is not to say that the political components of decision making can ever be completely overcome. For example, the possibility always exists that the criteria and associated information will be used to legitimize a priori decisions. Nonetheless, these tools reduce the likelihood of organizational paralysis and enable disparate units to argue the merits of various decisions based on shared values and information.

We present additional technical notes on the requirements for the development of a comparative information and resource system in the Appendix.

OVERCOMING CONSTRAINTS

Almost every organization needs to contend with constraints and interest group influences. In the absence of clearly articulated priorities and comparative information, however, higher education is especially vulnerable to such influences.

For example, the inability of administrators to lay off individual professors in the face of fiscal stress is often cited as a rationale for across-the-board cuts. If financial exigency is declared, tenure can be voided, and departments and professional schools can be targeted for elimination. However, declaration of financial exigency is seen as a declaration of bankruptcy. There are very few examples of such actions. In our view, the paralysis that declaration of financial exigency induces in decision makers outweighs its benefits. It is possible to eliminate departments or target them for reduction in size or restructuring without eliminating tenure. It is also possible to offer faculty in targeted units the option of moving to another department, early retirement, or voluntary separation options. The effectiveness of such strategies, however, requires that the institution (or system) establish and apply criteria for identifying priorities; in the absence of these decision-making criteria, fairly applied, efforts to overcome the constraints associated with tenure will be perceived as illegitimate and probably defeated.

The standards and evaluative criteria of the accrediting associations also constrain administrative action and may deter restructuring or reallocation efforts. Again, however, the absence of clearly articulated priorities, criteria for decision making about allocation decisions, and information about how disparate units fulfill these criteria, leaves central administration officials largely unable to justify actions directed toward reallocation or restructuring. If central administrators possess comparative evaluation criteria and supporting information when meeting with accrediting associations, the discussion might be more equal.

Interest groups also exert powerful influences over higher education policies ranging from admissions policies to partnerships with business. We know from the logic of collective action literature[8] that single-purpose groups are more effective in organizing and obtaining their goals than larger, multiple-purpose groups. In universities the only possible safeguard against private interests is more effective institutional arrangements that support university-wide goals as opposed to any particular set of interests. The development and application of the comparative decision-making evaluation criteria offer a beginning in the reestablishment of university-wide goals.

Guidelines for the Change Process

On the assumption that the changed environment requires reforms to existing governance systems, we present a set of inferences that are reasoned from the critique. Again, the inferences are based on the lessons learned by the present authors in carrying out academic planning and priority-setting efforts. Similar academic planning and priority-setting processes have been carried out in recent years at a number of major higher education institutions surveyed by the authors, including Wisconsin, University of California at Berkeley, Columbia, Stanford, and the University of Michigan. Here, then, are guidelines for higher education leaders to follow.

First, an improved governance system can be neither top-down nor bottom-up. Neither department-based solutions nor central administration solutions imposed from above are likely to succeed. A new governance system must be iterative; that is, the decision making needs to go both ways. Central administrators possess a broad perspective on systemic activities and functions. They must have the authority as well as the responsibility to set priorities and reallocate resources from low to high or new priorities among the units under their purview. They must provide the leadership to make the reform efforts work. But they will not be empowered to exercise this authority if the academic departments lack the opportunity to contribute to decision making. Only departments really know what their low and high or new priorities are. Consequently, academic departments must be integrally involved in the new governance system in a way that ensures they have as much of a stake in the governance system as the central administrators. This iterative process is critical to developing the capacity to establish priorities and criteria for decision making.

Second, even if department leaders accept the need for their institution to move beyond across-the-board cuts, they will be reluctant to cooperate unless they have guarantees and incentives as well as the threat of sanctions. This involves establishing a planning and priority-setting process viewed as legitimate by all participants. The planning process will vary from institution to institution or postsecondary system but will be comprised of the following rules of the game.

The planning and priority-setting process must be university-wide and everyone deemed eligible should be asked to participate on the same basis. This rule ensures that all academic and nonacademic units are subjected to the same comparative scrutiny from the standpoint of the university. Representatives of the units to be evaluated should be asked to help set the guidelines for the planning and priority-setting documents each unit submits to central administrators— that is, to deans or vice presidents. The statistical information to be collected and used should be agreed upon by participants, as well. Participants should also have a role in deciding the length of the planning and priority-setting process—on what date should it begin, when must preliminary documents be submitted, when must preliminary recommendations from the dean's or vice president's office be made, and so on.

Such a governance process envisages central administrators setting priorities and implementing them. However, academic units must be able to propose their plans and priorities and present supporting documentation. Because of the complexity of most higher education institutions and particularly because multiple goals and missions are pursued, it is important to build multiple review mechanisms into the planning effort. While central administrators must have final authority to make decisions, deans and vice presidents should appoint blue ribbon faculty committees from faculty assemblies to review and evaluate the planning documents that come forward. While central administrators may deviate from the recommendations of the faculty committees, these committees will provide a check on central administrators. To the extent the final decisions of central administrators follow the recommendations of the faculty committees, the legitimacy of the decisions is strengthened in the eyes of the faculty.

Third, the question of whether to conduct planning and priority-setting processes behind closed doors or to provide as much open information and discussion as possible is always debated at the start of such efforts. Openness brings with it negative publicity for any unit identified as a low priority. There are several persuasive arguments, however, for opting for openness. First, individual faculty members, departments, and colleges have legal and political avenues of redress available to them if they can argue they have not been given due process. Indeed, initial recommendations of faculty task forces and central administrators should be public and preliminary so as to allow affected units to rebut and reply. Thus appeal mechanisms must be put in place to allow a response by units that are affected by tentative recommendations. After all, the idea behind the new governance system is to set priorities, focus missions, and implement choices, not merely to create winners and losers. Achieving consensus on sharp, unevenly distributed cuts may sound impossible to deliver, but if the process is well designed, and if participants help design it and participate under rules developed through wide consultation among all levels of decision making, the institution may well accept the results.

In other words, we reject the idea that any one small group of decision makers alone can set priorities and reallocate resources in line with their own vision of the institution, a large and highly complex organization. Thus, the focus should be on creating the best possible process by which priorities can be set. Finally, institutions can improve even while reducing budgets and cutting back academic programs. If, for example, the missions of a higher education institution are more sharply focused, it may be easier to raise outside funds for an attractively defined set of missions. If at all possible, as well, academic units should be encouraged to put forward ambitious plans requiring increased funds for certain budget items while also listing low-priority items.

If the planning and priority setting process has been well designed, if the participants who help in designing it participate under rules developed through wide consultation among all levels of decision making in the higher education institution, the results are much more likely to be accepted by members of the institution. The members of the academic programs most negatively affected by the final recommendations may not agree, but the central administrators and senior faculty leaders can point to the fairness of the planning and priority setting process. Central administrators can then generate or retain support for the final recommendations from the faculty senates, assemblies, councils of deans and, of course, their own boards of trustees.

Some Implications of the Argument

In the end, the emphasis on department-based governance constitutes a fundamental barrier to the comparative, institution-wide allocation requirements of the new environment higher education faces today. The fundamental problem is a set of unquestioned assumptions or convictions shared by academics that translates into department-based governance of a logrolling quality. They are the following:

One, the ideology of universality or comprehensiveness which is widely regarded as a core operating assumption for universities. This translates into the view that all fields of knowledge—all the liberal arts and professional education—are equally valuable everywhere and at all times.

Two, the professionals organized around the structuring principle of a field of knowledge are the only ones equipped to govern themselves, decide what new subfields should be covered, what should be taught, and who should be hired, promoted, or fired. Outsiders, no matter how great their knowledge, skills, and accomplishments, lack the shared understanding needed to contribute effectively to such discussions.[9]

These convictions helped form the basic governance mechanism of the American university in the late nineteenth century—the department. And their continued sway might be all well and good if departments were truly autonomous, in financial as well as other ways.

But in reality they must function as parts of a greater whole—one on which they are financially dependent—and comparisons between academic departments and programs are essential for resource allocation and other aspects of governance.

The difficulty is that campus governance is somewhat like legislatures, with the departments equally divided into, say, six political parties. This governance system, when there are roughly equal votes, supports logrolling. Department x will tend to support department y's demands for hard-line positions in return for similar support from department y at a later date. There is every incentive to avoid college or university efforts to implement reallocation efforts because to do so means departments could lose control of at least a favorable status quo situation which protects them against losing positions. In the traditional growth era this was not as much of a problem because most departments continued to expand or at least not decline in resources. However, in the changed environment, the department-based governance threatens to create an academic version of Hardin's tragedy of the commons.[10] As total resources for the higher education institution decline, the incentive for each department is to strive even more to increase or keep its share of the budget. Under such circumstances, just as in Hardin's medieval village commons where the overall herd of cattle declined or died, the academic institution as a whole and its basic mission will dramatically deteriorate if the projected fiscal limits continue.

There are only two possible ways out of this academic version of the tragedy of the commons. First, in principle, a dictatorship could revive the academic commons. However, the discussion above suggests that such an effort would not be feasible in the American university at the end of the twentieth century. Any effort to exert a top-down solution to the prospective tragedy of the commons would run up against the entrenched decision-making rules of department-based governance. The only other feasible solution is more, not less, participation and much more sharing of comparative information, thus enabling participants to better understand the potential trade-offs of the resource allocation possibilities before them. Governance would be at the university level, the equivalent of the commons. However, all departments and other decision-making units would have to believe they not only had a stake in the outcome of decisions made but an opportunity to influence the outcome as well. Universities will probably have to move toward a flatter, better networked, decentralized governance structure above departments and below much of current central administration. Layers of deans and associate vice presidents will probably be eliminated over the next decade. Networks of faculty and administrators will replace them. Just how the new governance structure will be articulated will differ from one higher education institution to the next based on the particular historical development of each institution or system of institutions.

Appendix

NOTES FOR A COMPARATIVE INFORMATION AND RESOURCE SYSTEM TO ALIGN THE GOALS OF THE DEPARTMENT AND THE INSTITUTION

Institutions of higher education are striving to improve efficiency and effectiveness, but current information systems are fragmented and often inadequate. Resourcing systems focus on inputs (budget) not outputs, and performance cannot be effectively assessed, thus leading to a suboptimization of resources. In fact, many higher education institutions are experimenting with new techniques to reform their resource allocation mechanisms. New initiatives include responsibility-centered management, performance indicators, activity-based costing, business process redesign, and benchmarking. However, instead of being systematically integrated into the basic governance system of the institution, these initiatives are introduced in a piecemeal and marginal manner without sufficient consideration of the overall mission, objectives, and focus of the institution.

There needs to be a systematic and integrated system that guides the overall resource allocation structure of the higher education institution. We outline such a system and focus on one example, the need to align department activities with the institution's goals. Similar work needs to be done to align administrative activities with the institution's objectives. The system that we propose has at its apex

This appendix is based on field work in several university settings, not identified here, conducted by our RAND colleague Susan Way-Smith.

the overall objectives and mission of the institution. The activities of the institution, and in particular the activities of the institution's academic departments, support these objectives and missions. The information systems within the institution also support the activities and overall objectives. These systems must be flexible to adapt to changing objectives and must supply relevant decision-making information to the departments and the overall administrative structure.

The performance measures for the institution must also support its objectives and with the current and future resource limitations must be focused on outputs. These performance measures must be systematically used for all parts of the institution. The cost and quality measures are relatively self-explanatory. Flexibility is the ability of the institution to match its constituents' needs as they change over time. Time measures such as time taken to complete the degree are now critical in order to begin to ensure efficiency. The quality of the undergraduate education is also important to assess.

Finally, the institution must provide the incentives for individuals to support the institution's objectives. In reviewing the resourcing processes for several higher education institutions, we found that the factors used in resourcing create the wrong incentives for the institution. That is because departments tend to focus on expansion of their capacities at the cost of the overall institution. We also note that the subject of the incentives for faculty also requires examination.

The table below emphasizes the importance of the linkage between the department and the institution's overall missions and objectives. In this example, there is a mismatch between the activities of the department and the overall direction of the institution. The single department depicted is expending key instructional resources in elective areas at levels much higher than expended by the institution. The institution as a whole is more focused on required service courses and upper division majors and required courses for graduation.

In order to be sure department activities are aligned with overall institutional objectives, flexible and integrated bases that support development of the kind of information presented in Table 4.1 are needed. Unfortunately a department's instructional activities typically span several computerized information systems which are isolated from each other. In our pilot work to develop criteria for

Chart 4.1. Basic Elements of the Comparative Information and Resource System

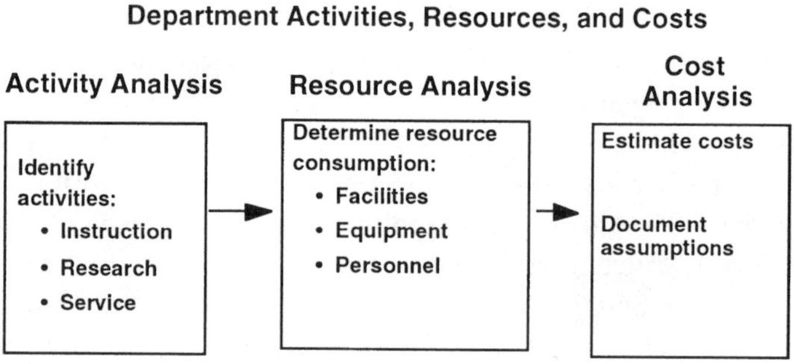

Department Activities, Resources, and Costs

Activity Analysis	Resource Analysis	Cost Analysis
Identify activities: • Instruction • Research • Service	Determine resource consumption: • Facilities • Equipment • Personnel	Estimate costs Document assumptions

Chart 4.2. An Integrated Database Facilitates Identification of Resource Consumption

Table 4.1. Departmental Activities Must Be Aligned with the Overall Institutional Objectives

Program	% Dept.	% Institution
Required grad. & U.D. majors courses	15	20
Required L.D. majors courses	20	20
Required service courses	5	20
High-priority elective courses—majors	30	20
Lower-priority elective courses—majors	25	10
G.E. courses	5	10

comparative information systems for two state universities, we found the following independent computer file databases for key data elements: enrollment, instructional staffing, support and administrative personnel, course sections, equipment costs, supply costs. Moreover, each database had different definitions for what appeared to be the same variables. And these definitions were not only inconsistent across these computer files but were also inconsistent across time within the same computer file for each key data element. Under such circumstances, it is impossible to know whether department activities are aligned with the institution's objectives.

What is ideally required is illustrated by Chart 4.2. Here one consolidates department activities, resources, and costs to give a picture of what is consuming the major resources and how that consumption might be changed by presenting cost estimates of resources consumed and the assumptions used to make the cost estimates. If the information suggested in Chart 4.2 were available, both department and university level observers could compare the department's use of resources with the institution's objectives. This is a necessary condition for institution-wide comparative-based resource allocation.

Notes

1. See Benjamin et al. (1993) for the general statement of the thesis argued here. Cf. Benjamin and Carroll (1997). This chapter should also be read in the context set by other recent general studies of the problems facing higher education, particularly Bensimon and Neuman (1993) and Gilmore (1992).

2. The data presented in this section are derived from a series published by the U.S. Department of Education (1995a) and U.S. Department of Education (1995b).

3. Rank-specific data on faculty salaries prior to 1965 are not readily available, but data from 1965 to 1995 have been provided by Research Associates of Washington.

4. We believe the recent cutbacks in public support to higher education are long-term in nature and not a function of the recent recession. The trend toward slower growth in public support to higher education was underway well before the current recession. Furthermore, this slowdown came not only at the federal level, but also at the state and local levels, reflecting the increased competition for public resources overall. Specifically, higher education's share of state revenues continued to decline relative to funding for prisons (+7.7%), Medicaid (+5.4%), and K-12 education (+7.3%) for financial year 1995. These calculations are based on statistics from the United States Department of Education (1995b). See also *The Finance Project and Center for the Study of the States* (1995).

5. See *Faculty of Arts and Sciences Undergraduate Catalogue* (1992).

6. One of the authors of this paper (Roger Benjamin) has participated in three exercises in university strategic planning each of which developed versions of these criteria listed in the same order of importance. An informal survey of strategic planning efforts in a number of other universities confirms this point. See University of Pittsburgh, *The University Plan* (1984) (1985). Cf. *College of Liberal Arts Planning Document* (1981). University of Minnesota.

7. For a review of the use of these comparative decision-making criteria see Clugston (1987).

8. See Olson (1965) and Benjamin (1980) for examples.

9. Benjamin and Carroll (1996): 20.

10. See Hardin (1968) for the original statement of the tragedy of the commons thesis.

References

Benjamin, R. (1980). *The Limits of Politics: Collective Goods and Political Change in Postindustrial Societies*. Chicago: University of Chicago Press.

Benjamin, R., S. Carroll, M. Jacobi, C. Krop, and M. Shires. (1993). *The Redesign of Governance in Higher Education*. Santa Monica: RAND, MR-222-LE.

Benjamin, R., and S. Carroll. (1996). "Impediments and Imperatives in Redesigning Higher Education." *Educational Administration Quarterly* 32 (Supplemental): 705–19. December.

Bensimon, E. M., and A. Neuman. (1993). *Redesigning Collegiate Leadership: Teams and Teamwork in Higher Education*. Baltimore, Md.: Johns Hopkins University Press.

Clugston, R. M., Jr. (1987). "Strategic Adaptation in An Organized Anarchy: Priority Setting and Resource Allocation in the Liberal Arts College of A Public Research University." Ph.D. diss., University of Minnesota, Twin Cities.

College of Liberal Arts (1981). *College of Liberal Arts Planning Document*. Minneapolis: University of Minnesota.

Faculty of Arts and Sciences Undergraduate Catalogue (1992). University of California at Los Angeles.

The Finance Project and Center for the Study of the States (1995). *State Investments in Education and Other Children's Services: Fiscal Profiles of the States*. Washington, D.C.: Finance Project.

Gilmore, J. L. (1992). "Evaluating Academic Productivity and Quality." In *Containing Costs and Improving Productivity in Higher Education*, ed. C. S. Hollins. San Francisco: Jossey-Bass.

Hardin, G. (1968, December 13). "The Tragedy of the Commons." *Science* 162: 1243–48.

Olson, M. (1965). *The Logic of Collective Action*. Cambridge: Harvard University Press.

Research Associates of Washington (1995). *Inflation Measures for Schools, College, and Libraries, Update*. Washington, D.C.

United States Department of Education, National Center for Education Statistics (1995a). *Digest of Educational Statistics: 1995*. Washington, D.C.: U.S. Government Printing Office.

——— (1995b). *Projections of Educational Statistics to 2005*. Washington, D.C.: U.S. Government Printing Office.

University of Pittsburgh (1984). *The University Plan: 1985–1990: Preliminary Recommendations*. Pittsburgh: Office of the Chancellor.

University of Pittsburgh (1985). *The University Plan: 1985–1990: Final Recommendations*. Pittsburgh: Office of the Chancellor.

5

Achieving High Performance: The Policy Dimension

PETER T. EWELL

🎓 🎓 🎓

DESPITE PERIODIC AND OFTEN VEHEMENT EPISODES OF DENIAL BY MEM-
bers of the academy, U.S. colleges and universities have always been
peculiarly public enterprises. Diversity and autonomy—prized by
most as unique features of the U.S. system of higher education—remain more the product of a characteristic national approach to structuring major social institutions than the result of specific public policy choices. But they are nevertheless shaped by a particular political
culture. Autonomy in particular has always been based on a substantial, though sometimes precarious, behavioral alignment between
societal ends and academic activities. It has emphatically not been
granted because academic activities are considered socially valuable
in themselves. In considering how institutions of higher education
can restructure themselves to achieve academic high performance,
recognizing this distinction is essential. And as they see continuing
erosion in the alignment between actions and purposes on which autonomy has historically been based, public officials have been quick
to call attention to it.

The result has been a decade of growing acrimony between the
academy and the wider society (Newman, 1987). Academic leaders,
attempting to build high-quality institutions along lines only recently
celebrated by the press and by popular opinion (and that still appear
highly regarded both by grantmakers and by the parents of potential students), cannot understand why the politicians have suddenly
turned vicious. All too often, they are ready to explain such reactions
simply as a matter of communication, believing that criticism would

cease if they could only find better ways to tell their stories (Ewell, 1994a). Public officials, in turn, are frustrated by what they see as a fundamental lack of responsiveness from academic institutions on an expanding set of issues that ranges from workplace skills to social ills. What they too often fail to see is that colleges and universities are responding to myriad incentives and payoffs that for the most part were put in place originally, and continue to be supported, by the actions of government.

Understanding the resulting dialectic is important because achieving high performance requires actions by both parties. First and most obviously, as Ellen Chaffee and William Tierney pointed out in Chapters One and Two, respectively, this is because what is most needed in instructional organization and pedagogy must be accompanied by a parallel restructuring of institutional assets and resources—most of which, regardless of formal control, remain overwhelmingly public. Those who have title to these assets and who allocate these resources must be fully engaged as partners in the process of transformation, or it will not succeed. More fundamentally, as Larry Braskamp and Jon Wergin have noted in Chapter Three, it is because high performance itself can only be defined by reference to societal needs and conditions. Changes in pedagogy that require active student engagement through problem-based exercises, that fuse the workplace and classroom through service learning, or that emphasize real confrontations with ethnic and social diversity, demand scrapping many artificial boundaries between universities and communities. They cannot be successful when societal contexts are treated merely as "settings" for the application of scholarship or discipline-based instruction. Alterations in basic instructional paradigms instead require full partnerships, both in understanding what is needed and in defining the terms of interaction.

This chapter argues that active public engagement on the part of all colleges and universities is a requisite for achieving academic high performance. At the same time, it maintains that considerable changes are required in higher educational policy, not just in institutional behavior, if active engagement is to occur. For practicing academic administrators, at a minimum, this requires three things. The first is a clear understanding about exactly what is wanted. Lying behind current political rhetoric are some real complaints, many of which change-minded members of the academy already agree with.

Yet these are rarely formulated in a manner concrete enough to develop specific alternatives in response. The first section of the chapter therefore attempts to sort out demands more clearly by arguing initially that American higher education looks the way it does precisely because it *has* responded to underlying social conditions, and subsequently by laying out systematically the particular domains of academic performance that appear to be dominating current external attention.

A second requirement is to recognize that real transformation demands changes in many of the ways government authorities themselves do business. To put it succinctly, "reinventing" higher education to achieve high performance requires a simultaneous effort to reinvent government itself, at least as it affects the ways colleges and universities are typically governed, funded, and evaluated. Driven by funding shortfalls and the increasingly apparent ineffectiveness of regulatory approaches to governing public enterprises in all fields, this is already happening (Osborne and Gaebler, 1992). But the resulting changes are scattered and have yet to be developed systematically into a new paradigm that relates public policy to higher learning (McTaggart and Associates, 1996). An important prerequisite for developing such a paradigm is to recognize explicitly some of the many characteristics of current policy approaches that actively block reform. The second section of the chapter reviews the most salient of these, then attempts a brief reformulation of the central thrusts of policy that might guide the development of a new governmental approach.

A final requirement for progress is to translate the resulting shift of perspective into a set of concrete changes in the specific policies that are most influential in shaping the environment for institutional behavior. The message here is that all such policy changes must be synchronous and mutually reinforcing, in strong contrast to the piecemeal pattern of past policy development in higher education. The chapter's third section thus examines in greater detail some of the implications of this new approach for the key arenas of higher education policy, including finance, the organization and "accounting" of instruction, and more general accountability.

Meeting these three requirements constitutes a major challenge for leadership, both within higher education and among policymakers committed to its support and development. But given the subtle but inescapably public character of American colleges and universities, it constitutes a necessary condition for achieving the promises outlined elsewhere in this volume.

Current Demands and Their Origins

The contention that U.S. higher education must be conceptualized and managed as a public enterprise appears dubious at first glance. Almost half of U.S. postsecondary institutions are private, and though they enroll fewer than a quarter of all students, such institutions exert disproportionate policy influence as well as dominating the public's image of "college." At the same time, the public sector is both diverse and decentralized, conditioned by the substantially different governance structures and funding commitments of the fifty states (McGuinness, 1994a). As a result, most public perception and scholarly argument has tended to emphasize the nonpublic character of the American postsecondary enterprise when compared to those of other nations. From a functional standpoint, however, it is equally important to emphasize the ways in which this loosely coupled system has historically been constructed by its surrounding society and politics and what has happened to it when it has not (Parsons and Platt, 1973). Before examining the roadmap of current societal demand, therefore, it is useful to look at this path of development more explicitly.

HIGHER EDUCATION AS A SOCIALLY CONSTRUCTED SYSTEM

Among the principal themes of U.S. postsecondary development for at least the past century-and-a-half have been a commitment to broad participation and an unusual degree of institutional diversification and market responsiveness. As in other social institutions during this period, these characteristics were admirably adapted to a rapidly developing yet locally centered capitalist polity and society. Unlike European universities, which tended to bolster the position of existing class-based elites (or to create new ones in the form of a class of intellectuals), the U.S. collegiate experience substantially encouraged participation as a matter of individual election and consumer choice. This, in turn, meant that niches evolved for all kinds of institutions, most of them small and highly parochial in character. This meant that colleges tended to evolve through explicit linkages with local regions and communities, often through common religious affiliation (Rudolph, 1977). This evolution strongly reinforced the development of autonomous institutions, which occasionally acted in concert to respond to emerging market forces (as in the creation of the first regional accrediting bodies at about the turn of the century), but operating for the most part as free-standing, self-governed units like the congregations that founded them. Unconscious but widely accepted policy goals for higher education during this period tended to emphasize individual benefit, but also included conscious socialization into a particular polity or community (Levine, 1978). Phrases like the "development of character" and "creating lives of service" in the current mission statements of most independent institutions remain legacies of these earlier communitarian purposes.

The publicly owned and publicly funded universities that began gradually to be added to this institutional mix in the mid-to-late nineteenth century, first through the major land grants but later in response to growing demands for teacher training, were largely intended as utilitarian from the outset (Keppel, 1991). Emphasizing agriculture, engineering, mining, and training in the professions, their activities were intentionally centered on fostering the kinds of practical arts required by a developing economy. Though much heralded as a landmark, the widespread reorganization of the major universities along Germanic lines in this period did not necessarily make them European universities (Perkin, 1984). Departmental and disciplinary structures evolved according to their own logic to be sure, but actual research and instructional programs remained visibly tied to market forces, application, and practice. Until the Second World War, U.S. higher education policy was thus deeply but unconsciously embedded in the design of individual institutions and their programs. Except for the many left out of the system (an exclusion applying to other social institutions as well) there was simply no need to coordinate an asset that for the most part was aligned with public purposes already.

The war and its aftermath was what really created the Germanic system of compartmentalized disciplines and departments. This transformation too was the result of political action. With a considerable scholarly asset in place, the logical course of action appeared to be to mobilize it, like any other industry, in support of national purposes. For almost two generations during the following cold war period large-scale federal support of basic research induced major changes in faculty culture and created a discipline-based system of scholarship on a national basis. The decision to continue to house this asset in university settings, rather than create free-standing research institutes as some nations did, also proved important because of the internal trade-offs that institutions made between instructional and research functions.

At the same time, the stage was set for an unprecedented expansion of support for the instructional component of the system, again primarily through government action. The GI Bill and creation of an extensive federal student assistance program two decades later were based initially on the grounds of individual social justice and later to develop a more productive national workforce (Eaton, 1992). States and the private sector, meanwhile, were expected to provide the increased instructional capacity needed to meet this growing market demand—an expansion which a rapidly growing economy, for a time, was able to support relatively easily. For the most part, however, the system grew along lines already established by the incentives in place. Full-time-equivalent (FTE)-based state funding formulas and federally underwritten tuition payments were sufficient to supplement and gradually subsidize an internal economy oriented primarily toward external research support. Even in colleges and universities that lacked substantial support of this kind, the resources of expansion were sufficient to underwrite the new faculty culture, which had grown quickly in the few large graduate schools that produced the majority of faculty but was often disconnected from the instructional missions originally assigned to these institutions.

This abbreviated, and admittedly revisionist, review of recent history makes the point that the structure of the U.S. system of higher education has always been fundamentally conditioned by identifiable social choices and deliberate political actions. The system in place is a *constructed* system—the product of created values and incentives—that can equally be remade by consciously altering these values and incentives. As such changes are contemplated, however, it is well to recall at least three premises which this path of development also suggests and which will continue to condition the impact of policy on higher education in the future:

1. *Effective action is indirect.* Changes in the structure and practices of U.S. colleges and universities have always been driven far more by incentives and markets than by regulations and mandates. Recent attempts to reform institutions by direct action, like the establishment of minimum standards for student achievement or mandated faculty workload policies, will have little impact without parallel changes in the incentive structures on which current behaviors rest.

2. *The "hidden hand" of market forces and incentive structures, while it affects institutions individually, nevertheless defines a national system.* On the one hand, this means that independent actions taken by individual institutions to restructure internally are unlikely to be sustainable without simultaneous attention to realigning incentives more generally. On the other hand, it emphasizes that policy action, however indirect, does have a long-term impact.

3. *Both instruction and scholarship in the United States can be publicly sustained only if they continue to center themselves broadly on the practical arts.* Neither now nor in the past has U.S. society had much use for a class of intellectuals, either as the inhabitants or the products of its colleges and universities. Scholarship is at its most sustainable when guided by the metaphor of practical invention which remains deeply embedded and respected in the nation's values. Similarly, the principal objects of instruction will always be seen by the public as employment and civic contribution, not academic mastery per se.

These basic premises of policy are too often forgotten by those who seek either to preserve or transform the academy from within. Recognizing their continuing relevance in the context of a changing pattern of public demand remains critical to achieving high performance in the current context.

THE EMERGING PATTERN OF DEMAND

Many observers now recognize that academic and political leaders have been talking past one another for about a decade. To some extent, this condition is natural, reflecting markedly different ends, values, and backgrounds. But it is also a product of the way such communication has typically been handled on both sides. Inside institutions, disengagement from issues of public concern on the part of both administrators and faculty is often by mutual consent. In a noble attempt at protection, administrators have largely shielded faculty from political impact. Faculty, for their part, remain happy to delegate to others the task of justifying what they do. Faced with the resulting lack of engagement, political leaders are growing dangerously certain that continuing uphill attempts to persuade higher education to become more responsive may not be worth the trouble (Ruppert, 1996). As a result, they are tempted simply to turn their backs on the enterprise and cease to invest in it. Growing interest in private technology-based alternatives to existing institutions and in fostering "school-to-work" arrangements that "end-around" higher education for a large number of citizens are early signs of this conviction.

To get behind current criticisms and examine the real messages that political leaders are sending first requires understanding what they see as the problem. While the rhetoric here often centers on quality, the specific performance of colleges and universities has rarely been the real focus of concern. Unlike K–12 education, where the actual products of the system and how to improve them form the core of the discussion, higher education's accountability problem throughout the last decade has always been more a crisis of confidence about the ability of the enterprise to manage itself responsively and to respond appropriately to public needs and concerns (Ewell, 1990). Somewhat ironically, moreover, the lack of a visible quality problem means that higher education is simply not seen as broken enough to demand increased attention, compared to such massive challenges as reforming elementary / secondary education or restructuring the nation's health care and criminal justice systems. This structural condition alone leads to miscommunication, as academics can argue quite rightly that nothing is wrong with performance, while policy leaders can find few alternatives to tightening accountability measures in order to call attention to what they see as a completely different set of issues.

External voices, however, have been neither consistent nor coherent in advocating new policy approaches. Indeed, they have shown a sometimes exasperating tendency to cling to traditional policy mechanisms that are in fact badly suited to inducing institutions to behave in new ways (McGuinness, 1996). Among these are frequent reversions to the language of efficiency which emphasizes short-term cost-savings rather than fundamental restructuring, narrow institution-based accountability which ignores joint products and systemic concerns, and the understandably political desire to protect the interests of locally based institutions. The pervasive quality of these linguistic reversions—partly a product of the fact that a new policy language to frame what is needed has yet to evolve—makes it hard for academic audiences to see current criticisms as anything more than politics as usual (Ewell, 1994a).

Clear communication is also masked by a curious rhetorical dialectic embedded in much public criticism. On the one hand, reflecting broad public sentiment, political comment about higher education's performance implies a good deal of residual deference, continuing to emphasize prestige, preserving traditional norms and structures, and the protection of an elite status for public universities. This is the image of college which legislators understand best, and the erosion of which they quite rightly perceive as a concern of the most expressive of their constituents. On the other hand, it is often precisely these institutions that make them most angry, both because of the sheer frustration experienced in getting the attention of these institutions and, at a deeper and darker level, because of a profound anti-intellectualism that they know their constituents share.

Despite these considerable rhetorical obstacles, at least three concrete demands pervade the current pattern of external comment. The first centers on achieving efficiencies without undermining quality, an objective advanced not just as cost-cutting, but with the knowledge that virtually every other U.S. enterprise has had to do the same. The second enjoins higher education to become more customer oriented, especially in serving an increasingly diverse and demanding student population, but advocating greater responsiveness to the needs of employers and communities as well. The final theme emphasizes turning the assets of scholarship, bought with public dollars, toward the solution of immediate, identifiable social problems.

Demands to Live within Means

Perhaps the most fundamental misunderstanding between policymakers and academics concerns the future availability of resources. While many college leaders recognize that economic difficulties lead to short-term troubles, few remain ready to admit (and still less to plan for) serious threats to what they see as higher education's manifest destiny of continued expansion (Ewell, 1994b). Meanwhile, their strategy is to protect core assets (chiefly in the form of full-time faculty), with the expectation that the temporarily cut periphery (chiefly plant and equipment, support services, libraries and part-time people) can be quickly made up when funding is restored. At the same time, they tend to see current cuts as actively punitive, a product of ignorant ill-will on the part of politicians who neither understand nor value the academic enterprise.

In contrast, current funding levels for public higher education are the product of fundamental structural conditions. In the majority of states, expenditures on higher education have become the budget balancer, the major piece of discretionary spending remaining after mandatory expenditures such as court-ordered K–12 equalization funding or required state-level matching for increasingly expensive federal programs like Medicaid are deducted. A second element of this structural equation is the fact that taxpayers simply will not support further increases. Demands on higher education are also going up. Many states now face the prospect of accommodating substantial increases in enrollment, beginning at about the turn of the new century. Finally, employers are insisting on more and better preparation for an adaptive, responsible, and teachable workforce to help meet the competitive realities of a global economy. The academy is quite right to see the resulting pattern as a demand to do more for less. But it is wrong to see it as a demand for efficiency alone.

To those outside higher education, in contrast, this combination of structurally induced fiscal stringency in the face of an increasingly demanding customer is quite familiar, vividly recalling the operating environment of U.S. industry over the last two decades. Fundamental to this environment is a demand for quality service delivered at reduced provider cost, a conceptual linkage that, until recently, higher education has been slow to grasp. Public policymakers are well aware that restructuring in public enterprises like K–12 education and health care is being fueled by the basic recognition that current modes of operation, however efficient they can be made, cannot provide the savings required. In contrast, they see higher education demanding that each new responsibility be treated as an add-on, requiring a new and independent budget line, but with little or no impact on wider organizational forms and functions (Pew Higher Education Research Program, 1990).

Contrary to popular belief within the academy, such concerns are often expressed most visibly by those who have been higher education's greatest champions in state legislatures and governors' offices. On the one hand, they feel that academic leaders have provided them with little evidence of engagement or of results obtained that they can use as ammunition in increasingly contentious budget debates. On the other hand, they are plagued with a range of specific complaints centering on apparently low faculty workloads and excessively long student times to graduation, issues which are related to, but do not adequately expose, the real productivity dilemma. As a result, key policy makers are increasingly likely to resort to mandates that are directed at these specific manifestations of the problem, if only to get something moving.

Demands to Become More Educationally Responsive

Commonly expressed external criticisms about faculty workload must be similarly dissected to reveal what lies behind them. Certainly, such concerns have become widespread, with more than two dozen states engaged in investigations of faculty work or the development of new statistical indicators to monitor it. Rather than being simply reactive or anti-intellectual, however, such actions reveal deeper policy concerns. One motivation centers on pure efficiency, as was also the case in the mid-seventies when the standard technologies to account for faculty time were developed. But in many ways, as William Tierney noted in Chapter Two, policy makers are less worried about how hard faculty are working than they are about what students are getting as a result.

If cost constitutes the principal political point of entry into issues of higher education, student experiences and outcomes remain its inescapable bottom lines. And since about the mid-eighties, the volume of complaints about both has been on the rise. Most of these center less on faculty actions than on the ways public colleges and universities treat students more generally. Inflexible and incomprehensible administrative procedures, the inability to get needed classes in a timely fashion, and lack of attention to providing help in navigating the bureaucratic superstructure that surrounds the typical undergraduate experience dominate attention here. As a result, squandered student time is as much the political focus of concern as misdirected faculty effort (Education Commission of the States [ECS], 1995). Indeed, it is often astounding to external observers that, unlike successful businesses, colleges and universities fail to include customer time as a variable in the productivity equation at all.

Many in the policy community are also aware of the profound changes that have already been implemented in public K–12 classrooms. Familiar with such K–12 concepts as active learning, peer-based learning communities, and authentic assessment, they wonder why they see little of these concepts in higher education (Ruppert, 1996). It is not surprising, therefore, that a major motif of the current policy agenda for higher education is consumer protection. The most recent state-based accountability initiatives, for example, tend to emphasize improving students' ability to comparison shop by insisting that institutions provide concrete information about the kinds of services that they can expect and the kinds of jobs and skills that they will possess after graduation (ECS, 1995). And as students are asked to shoulder a growing share of the costs associated with attendance, requiring institutions to disclose such information is seen as increasingly legitimate.

That employers as well as students are concerned about outcomes is equally important. Most, however, have few complaints about the results of graduate training or of instruction in the major field. Instead they have become increasingly vocal about the need for a common set of crosscutting attributes in college-level people they employ, regardless of technical or professional proficiency (ECS, 1995; Ewell, 1995; Gardiner, 1994). Among the most commonly mentioned attributes are facility in oral communication, problem-solving skills (especially in ill-specified situations), high motivation and a sense of professional responsibility, and the ability to work effectively in teams. Most of these attributes are as much about character as about cognition, and virtually all of them emphasize application over knowledge.

Responding explicitly to these clear customer interests constitutes a major current test of higher education's credibility. But policy makers are generally far less concerned about the specific means used to respond to these interests than whether they are being heard in the first place. Mandates intended to redirect workload or to dictate pedagogy tend to occur less because such actions are considered by policy makers to be appropriate or even effective than because these tests of basic credibility are not met.

Specific Demands for Assistance and Partnership

Added to general concerns about lack of responsiveness in the core function of instruction are some far more specific demands to deploy higher education's assets toward helping to address particular social problems. This imperative, of course, hearkens back to what policy makers thought they were buying when they built the land-grant colleges. Lack of response to it, in turn, helps fuel frustration because the academic enterprise is seen as deliberately avoiding what the key members of the public see as a basic assignment. Larry Braskamp and Jon Wergin's Chapter Three discusses one possible response that policy makers may seek, but we should note the struggles that come about when we seek to change faculty work.

A prominent case in point is providing assistance to K–12 education. Most policy makers believe that elementary and secondary education is in trouble but is taking active steps to deal with its many problems (Ruppert, 1996). At the same time, they see little active engagement toward addressing these problems by public higher education, which constitutes both the predominant supplier of future K–12 teachers and the educational destination of nearly half of K–12 products. Where such engagement does occur, it tends to be confined to Schools of Education, under terms dictated largely by the requirements of faculty scholarship. True partnerships in which faculty drawn from both higher and lower education attempt to address common problems of student preparation on a subject-by-subject basis remain relatively rare. The external audience does not see the same depth of commitment to change in higher education as it does in lower education. A wide transformation of values and incentives will obviously be required in colleges and universities. Similar points can be made about applied research and the long neglected service missions of public institutions. Indeed, the meaning of the word *service* itself has drifted significantly in recent years, from active engagement with external agencies to the inwardly focused role of faculties in university governance. One result has been to reinforce the growing isolation of most institutions from their surrounding communities. Research, in turn, is most aligned with public purposes when it addresses problems that are both visible and local. Elementary / secondary education again provides a broadly applicable example, but additional instances vary significantly from region to region: youth violence for institutions located in major urban areas, synthetic materials development in the rebuilding automotive industrial areas of the Midwest, or tertiary oil recovery in the Rocky Mountain West.

Redirecting higher education's research and service capacities toward public purposes in this fashion requires state governments to systematically create markets for specific research and service activity, much as the federal government did for basic research during the three decades after Sputnik, but on a far more local basis (Richardson, 1996).

An appropriate response to this emerging constellation of demands requires more than just increased communication between academic and political constituencies. Like any form of cross-cultural exchange, it requires new vocabularies and detailed recognition of the operating realities that govern both academic institutions and government bodies. Better listening on both sides is surely needed. But making progress will require more explicitly re-visioned approaches to policy, as well as a clearer recognition of what is wrong with the majority of policies now in place.

Developing New Metaphors for Policy

A particularly pernicious implication of recent debates about realigning higher education with public purposes is that colleges and universities are expected to do all the changing. Not only does this ignore the fact that the actions of higher education institutions are consistent with incentives and constraints previously established by policy, but it also frames the issue in terms ill-suited to fostering a lasting partnership. We need new ways to conceptualize the entire relationship, recognizing that the structure and implementation of policy itself must change, and with it the way governments do business.

A first condition for remaking policy metaphors is to explicitly acknowledge some widespread syndromes of higher education policy that continue to block institution-level reform. Many of these are subtle and pervasive, characterizing not just higher education policy but the wider state structures and the political cultures that sustain such policy. A second requirement is to develop new ways to conceptualize policy relationships that avoid these syndromes. Fundamental to both, in turn, is understanding the limits of government action in shaping academic behavior and what kinds of actions are effective in this regard.

SOME SYNDROMES OF CURRENT HIGHER EDUCATION POLICY

Some general attributes of current governance, funding, and regulatory policies profoundly affect the capacity of colleges and universities to innovate. At the same time, each state constitutes a unique political culture whose specific features will influence the degree to which these syndromes are present and will determine the particular forms in which they occur. Any effort to restructure policy should therefore begin with a thorough analysis of the distinctive ways each state's constellation of policies and culture act in concert to induce or inhibit desired institutional behaviors (Jones and Ewell, 1993).

Many state policies affecting higher education are also characterized by a wider approach to government that combines an emphasis on citizen access to public benefits with a long-standing concern about efficiency (McGuinness, 1994b). Regional differences and urban-rural tensions can create an additional need to balance disparate interests in the day-to-day practice of politics. One result in most states is that it is extremely difficult to develop policies that do not contain "something for everybody"—an outcome that often negates the clarity of original policy intent. Another result is strong pressure to embed such compromises in centralized compacts that apply equally to all parties. The actual content of the resulting policies thus tends to hide these underlying differences from everybody except those involved in the original bargaining. The equitable promulgation and enforcement of these policies, in turn, tend to block legitimate attempts to develop unique and locally appropriate solutions. In addition to these general characteristics, some specific attributes of current policy actively inhibit the kinds of institutional initiatives needed to achieve high performance (National Center for Higher Education Management Systems [NCHEMS], 1994). Among them are the following:

— policies designed principally to prevent bad things from happening rather than to enable good things to happen.

A basic assumption underlying most regulatory action is that without close control, those charged with executing public purposes will ignore them and those spending state dollars will waste them. While widely cited as being out of touch with emerging management styles that emphasize broad direction setting and decentralized management practice, this syndrome remains strongly entrenched in many statehouses. Among its specific manifestations are the following:

- policy approaches that actively punish institutional behaviors, either fiscally or through the application of sanctions, rather than providing positive incentives for colleges and universities to behave in desired ways.

- legislation and regulation designed to prevent a particular incident or action from ever occurring again by placing specific limits on or detailed oversight over institutional procedures.

- policies that emphasize checking lower-level decisions and plans to ensure that they comply with detailed regulations and guidelines.

Emerging experience suggests strongly that such approaches to policy tend to create exactly the kinds of institutional behaviors that they are intended to prevent. Faced with rules, campuses work to rule. More and more, they will attempt to second-guess the system, with escalating levels of cynicism as they do so, further eroding the kinds of active partnership needed to address public concerns.

— a one-size-fits-all approach to policy development and implementation that fails to recognize or accommodate legitimate differences between institutional circumstances, characteristics, and clienteles.

A prominent root of this syndrome among policy makers is a lack of familiarity with such diversity. This often results in a subtle tendency to build policy as though all students are four-year, full-time attenders; to assume that all institutions are organized and operate like traditional residential campuses; and to generalize to all its public institutions problems and phenomena that occur principally at the state's flagship campus. Reinforcing this problem is the common failure to provide an underlying rationale for developing a particular policy, nor is advice on its implementation sought from the institutions that it affects. This effectively precludes campuses or operating units from having the opportunity to propose creative alternatives that can accomplish intended policy objectives consistent with local conditions. Some of the most prominent instances of such overly uniform applications of policy are the following:

- cutting-across-the-board approaches to budget reduction that fail to recognize important differences between campuses with respect to fixed and variable costs, or their relative abilities to generate economies of scale. This approach is most apparent under conditions of budgetary decline and is also typical of budget expansion in good years.
- uniform implementation of policies like early retirement, caps on tuition, or restrictions on specific types of expenditures that have markedly different impacts on different campuses because of structural or historic variations in staffing patterns and student populations.
- the application of prevention-oriented rules and procedures to all institutions, regardless of their individual records of actually experiencing the kinds of problems that led to these regulations in the first place.

This syndrome in many ways parallels the essential dilemmas involved in remaking faculty roles and rewards at the institutional level. Both require the ability to accept rational inconsistencies in the ways units or individuals are treated within a broader rubric of clear collective goals and results-oriented standards of achievement.

— administrative structures and behaviors that treat colleges and universities simply as state agencies.

For the most part, these embrace regulations and procedures that are outside the control of state higher education agencies. Their primary impact at the campus level is to create extreme disincentives for operating entrepreneurially, which is arguably how colleges and universities work best. The most common include the following:

- state personnel systems for classified employees that limit the ability to build teams, to reward initiative, or to sanction lack of productivity. Such impacts also apply to both instructional and noninstructional personnel in collective bargaining settings. A particular problem in the latter case is the tendency for proposed innovations to be bargained up to a central authority for final decision, making it extremely difficult to build local cross-functional partnerships to address common problems.

• constraints on outsourcing or external contracting that prevent institutions from obtaining services like facilities maintenance, transportation, or computing services from local vendors, often at lower costs and with higher quality.

• limits placed on mission-related service or contractual activities (often in the name of curbing unfair business competition with local businesses or services) that actively prevent institutions from discharging client requests for partnership.

• the need to file numerous compliance reports according to state agendas that are uncoordinated in schedule and purpose and that use inconsistent definitions of key terms.

Such factors often render officially granted autonomy more statutory than real by restricting substantially each institution's ability to make local decisions that will best meet varying conditions. State higher education authorities, despite their best efforts, often entirely counterbalance the effect of other policies explicitly designed to give colleges and universities more freedom of action:

— treating state higher education agencies as regulators of individual institutional behaviors rather than as vision creators for the state's system of higher education as a whole.

The vast majority of the State Higher Education Executive Officers (SHEEO) agencies typically assigned responsibility for coordinating postsecondary education function either as institutional advocates or as government watchdogs. Few such entities are charged with taking a broad view of statewide needs and how higher education might meet them (McGuinness 1994b). Partly as a result, there is typically little communication about initiatives of common interest among different governing boards (most states have at least two) and little effort to convene institutional leaders on a statewide basis to address problems of mutual interest. The absence of a widely accepted agenda for higher education means that each institution pursues its own agenda. Under such conditions, the predominant role of statewide agencies becomes one of brokering conflicting interests between institutions, in contrast to creating active consensus around a set of policies consistent with state priorities (McGuinness, 1996). Specific manifestations of this syndrome follow:

— policies that are generally reactive to specific issues rather than being developed proactively to further deliberately chosen statewide plans or priorities.

— policies that are developed piecemeal, that do not fit together well, or that create incentives that actively conflict with one another. In many states, for example, initiatives designed to maintain access and promote success among historically deprived populations (e.g. targets for minority graduation) are inconsistent with funding mechanisms that systematically shift resources away from needed developmental and support services.

— no overall rationale for the current array of policies that either institutions or the public can understand. The original good intent of a given policy thus often becomes invisible once it is implemented, and few opportunities are available to explain how it should operate or what it was intended to do.

— little appreciation of the need to discontinue specific policies or initiatives when they have in fact achieved their principal purposes for the majority of institutions.

— The collective result of this condition is usually to confine agency activity to narrowly fiscal matters. Fostering active cooperation and joint ventures among institutions to address a common problem or to serve an identified regional need becomes especially difficult under these conditions. At the same time, state agencies themselves are under significant strain, caused by the same combination of circumstances now plaguing institutions (McGuinness, 1994a). Funding cuts stimulated by wider deregulatory impulses have significantly reduced staffing levels at most such agencies (and three states have abolished them in the last two years). Without a clear change in assignment, most agencies lack the means to discharge traditional administrative or regulatory functions effectively. This, in turn, further constrains institutional initiative because it tends to substantially slow the bureaucratic turnaround time needed to process new program requests or approve institutional budgets and plans.

Taken together, policy syndromes such as these create a network of structures and incentives that actively blocks institutional innovation. Well-intentioned attempts to alter the way institutions work internally will fail unless simultaneous attention is directed toward restructuring the wider environment within which they must operate.

FOUNDATIONS FOR A NEW POLICY PARADIGM

Developing specific approaches to policy designed to enhance academic high performance involves simultaneous attention to internal and external environments. On the one hand, it requires public policy makers to determine a good deal more precisely the kinds of behaviors that they want institutions to exhibit. On the other hand, it demands a coherent and articulated set of policy mechanisms designed to communicate these outcomes clearly and to allow institutions maximum flexibility in attaining these objectives (McTaggart and Associates, 1996).

Shifting the Axis of Institutional Attention

A fundamental premise for evolving such an alternative is that institutions and faculty already possess many of the necessary conditions for effecting internal transformations. Missing are the organizational structures and rewards that are needed to move their behavior in desired directions. Large-scale disciplinary research activities, for instance, are already collective and highly entrepreneurial. Their primary unit of organization is a diverse faculty team, governed by a strong sense of voluntary internal discipline, organized flexibly in pursuit of specific collective goals. The quality of the resulting product, in turn, is assessed in common through peer review, a form of collective judgment that, when it works well, has proven both rigorous and responsible. Rewards return to the team and benefit collectively all who participate.

An important domain of current faculty practice thus already appears consistent with reinvented organizational behaviors. The problem, of course, is just how consistently these elements align with societal needs and expectations. Although they are collective, research priorities are set within the academy and they tend in the main to reinforce existing discipline-based structures and values. The areas most frequently cited by the public and its elected representatives as needing higher education's attention, in contrast, are equally corporate in nature. But they require faculty to engage in collective action against the grain of current organizational and incentive structures.

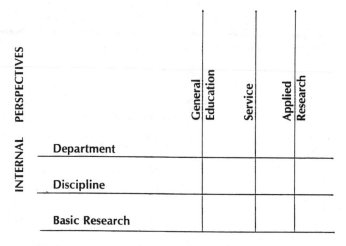

Figure 5.1. Shifting the Axis of Institutional Attention

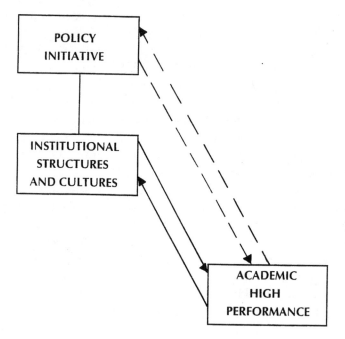

Figure 5.2. Shifting the Object of Policy Action

Given this situation, Figure 5.1 illustrates the shift in the axis of institutional attention that is required, from largely internal discipline-related matters to principally external customer-oriented areas of interest. Improving lower-division undergraduate general education, for example, is a common concern expressed by external publics, especially as it relates to the development of crosscutting practice-oriented abilities among students and the adoption of student-centered educational good practices by institutions. Other prominent examples of external priorities center on applied research and service in support of specific, identified social problems. Both kinds of examples are strongly cross-disciplinary in nature, as well as requiring collective commitment and activity to be successful. Given the nascent entrepreneurial tendencies already possessed by most faculties, the needed academic management trick lies less in redefining faculty work than in creating fiscal and structural environments through which these tendencies can be more effectively channelled.

Shifting the Object of State-Level Action

Many of the foundations for a revisioned approach to the development and implementation of state-level higher education policy are also already in place. Most recently, a strong climate of deregulation has reduced substantially the detailed oversight responsibilities of many higher education agencies. Those that have not been restructured have been severely constrained by significant staffing and resource shortfalls. But such developments can only establish the preconditions for evolving new state policy roles.

Changing the object of state policy first requires recognizing how far removed from institutional action state policy makers really are. As Figure 5.2 suggests, state policy has only a limited direct impact on educational practices and faculty behaviors (Jones and Ewell, 1993). But it can effectively shape both through its impact on institutional structures, incentives, and cultures. As the figure also suggests, it is quite possible for policy makers to end-run the influences of institutional structure and culture by initiating and rewarding institutional actions directly. This occurred frequently in the 1980s, particularly in the form of incentive grants designed to improve undergraduate education, and it proved an effective way to call needed attention to an issue or to initiate action (Berdahl and Holland, 1989). But later evaluation of such programs also suggested that the new ideas readily fostered by such pilots were not sustainable without more basic changes in institution-level structures and rewards. Consistent with the four basic syndromes of current policy noted earlier, the figure finally emphasizes the need to explicitly confront the incentive system already in place. Recognizing that the real initiative for change resides at the faculty/department level, the pertinent question for policy makers is the extent to which existing state policies and other factors serve as barriers to appropriate changes that will arise naturally at the local level with the proper incentives. In this sense, the issue is not so much how the state can promote transformation through proactive policy as it is one of how it can stay out of the way of faculty and institutional leaders once an appropriate set of structures and incentives is in place (McGuinness, 1994b).

This first suggests that the guiding metaphor for developing policy must change from one of coordinating and overseeing institutions to one of making and manipulating markets. Inspection of this phrasing reveals that both the activity and its object have been altered. On the one hand, the emphasis of policy action changes from direct (though generally reactive) intervention to establishing and consistently rewarding specific behaviors. Rather than checking up on local action after the fact, policy action is up front and is deliberately designed to be indirect. Another implication is that the primary referent of policy focuses less on the actions of individual institutions than on the ways multiple institutions act together to form an effective system. Under this rubric, crosscutting educational functions like effective and transferable undergraduate learning or problem-driven research and service become the primary object of policy attention, not colleges and universities as institutions.

A final implication of this shift is that policy action is focused principally on reinforcing and empowering institutional leadership. Returning to the logic of Figure 5.1, individual presidents and provosts are usually quite interested in initiating programs and activities that cross established organizational lines within their own institutions. Indeed, this is the only way they can make their mark as academic leaders. But they too are working against the grain of strongly established and highly decentralized resource allocation and decision-making processes. Substantial experience with both addition-to-base-funding incentive programs and state-level assessment mandates throughout the last decade suggests that external incentives can be of considerable value here. Using the momentum and resources provided by such incentives, creative campus leaders can use them to help sustain their own agendas while claiming that the institution has no choice but to follow them. Indeed, evaluations have commonly found that university leaders publicly oppose such state-level initiatives while privately expressing strong support for them (NCHEMS, 1992a).

Taken together, these two major shifts—from internal disciplinary matters to external customer-oriented concerns and from having the state develop proactive policies to having the state foster action on campuses—imply a particular approach to the way needed changes can best be managed within the current political arena, one that recognizes and harnesses existing forces and materials, and shapes them indirectly to create new patterns. As the following section delineates, making changes in each traditional element of state action, including finance, accountability, and programmatic oversight, is important. But realigning the overall policy design in terms of which of these individual ingredients interrelate is equally important.

Some Specific Implications for Policy

The vast majority of current state-level policies and structures for higher education evolved from a tradition of the state directly subsidizing and controlling individual public colleges and universities. Many were established during periods of dramatic growth some thirty years ago, largely in response to concerns about the unplanned proliferation and unnecessary duplication of new campuses and high-cost programs. Underlying large numbers of these policies were also efforts to protect particular sectors or institutions, or to help curb emerging and highly politically sensitive areas of competition among economic regions and demographic groups within each state.

Many of these concerns are still present. But it is apparent that some of the most basic assumptions under which these policies were originally designed are now obsolete. Consistent with the shifts in guiding metaphor noted above, a growing dialogue about new state roles in shaping higher education policy is emerging (SHEEO, 1989). Some of its specific themes for state action include the following:

— defining a consistent public agenda that connects the actions of a state's entire array of postsecondary resources to the needs of its most important clients.
— engaging in targeted strategic investment designed to further this agenda and to enhance the capacity of institutions to serve state needs through the incentives established by a managed market rather than the dictates of a command economy.
— aligning all current mechanisms that allocate funds to public institutions, as well as providing student assistance funds, in a way that maximizes market leverage on behalf of statewide interests.
— redefining institutional licensure, program authorization, and consumer-protection policies to emphasize outcomes rather than inputs and resources.
— phasing out increasingly obsolete definitions of institutional missions based on geographic service regions.
— establishing explicit incentives for cooperation among colleges and universities, and between them and other public institutions (such as schools, libraries, corporations, and government agencies), in order to create joint ventures that further public purposes.

A policy structure capable of doing such things requires a serious examination of the role played by each of the several "levers of change" that have always been in the hands of state leaders (Ewell, 1985). Prominent among these, expressed in established categories, are resource allocation and fiscal policy, the review and approval of individual academic programs, regulation and accountability reporting, and statewide master planning. Under newer and more appropriate labels, each of these functions has a part to play in a redesigned policy environment.

REMAKING RESOURCE ALLOCATION

In view of the much-vaunted power of the purse, it is somewhat surprising that state-level resource allocation mechanisms in higher education have only rarely been used to deliberately shape institutional behaviors. Most current budgeting mechanisms date back to higher education's great period of expansion in the late 1960s and early 1970s, when the principal imperative was simply to fund increases in capacity. The average-cost funding formulae that were built at that time, and which are still used by about half the states, were admirably suited to this purpose (Brinkman, 1984, Ahumada, 1990). Not only did they provide direct payoffs to institutions for individual expansion, but the they were constructed to provide general operating support rather than being directed toward funding particular functions. This feature allowed institutions to keep any benefits realized by increasing economies of scale (Jones, 1984). But the essential logic of these budgeting mechanisms, like those associated with any public utility, was one of cost-recovery rather than intentionally directed investment. On the one hand, this meant that institutional activities (chiefly accounted in terms of the number of students served) became the primary focus of institutional attention, not the original policy ends to be attained (for example, a more literate society and a more productive workforce). More insidiously, it implied that these accounted costs were both real and immutable, and that doing anything more would therefore cost more as well. Both features were used liberally by colleges and universities throughout the 1970s and 1980s to further their own agendas.

Remaking resource allocation consistent with the metaphor of making and manipulating markets first implies funding ends and functions rather than institutions and line items. Externally sponsored research, for example, differs decisively from the remainder of the current academic enterprise in the way the dollars flow. In the former, a client is funded, and providers must organize to deliver what is wanted to obtain funds from the client. In the latter, the providers are funded directly, with the hope that they will act as required. Academic institutions currently consist overwhelmingly of provider-funded reward structures, with the bulk of the regular budget allocated to permanently established units and departments. Within such structures, substantive change occurs only on a voluntary and consensual basis. Alternatively, it must be induced directly through external regulation and control (NCHEMS, 1992b; Jones, 1995).

Shifting resource allocation structures to more directly fund higher education clients represents one way to deliberately create a market designed to induce such changes. For example, a portion of the state's higher education budget might be allocated to each of its major geographic regions, or to a visible client group such as K–12 education, in order to provide them with the capacity to purchase back services consistent with their own needs on a competitive basis from the state's higher education institutions (or, indeed, from any other provider). Elements of Ohio's "Selective Excellence" program in the mid-1980s (NCHEMS, 1992a), and more recent proposals for implementing priority-based funding arrangements in Colorado (NCHEMS, 1992b) are consistent with this logic. Current high-tuition/high-aid proposals, though not explicitly designed to do so, put market leverage into the hands of individual students in a similar fashion.

Alternatively, the state can enter the market directly on its own behalf. This first requires clear identification of the specific public purposes to be achieved through intervention, a process that needs considerable consensus building with stakeholders to be effective (NCHEMS, 1994). Typical results of such a process include the development of broad-based goals that affect all institutions. In Colorado, for instance, the improvement of undergraduate general education and the use of improved instructional technology were specifically identified for targeted funding of this kind as part of a legislatively mandated priority-setting exercise (NCHEMS, 1992b). Other kinds of priorities include specific workforce or regional needs. Strategic funding models developed in New Jersey and Hawaii in recent years identified the particular service needs of underserved geographical areas for priority attention, while similar mechanisms under consideration in Wyoming are aimed at improving tertiary oil recovery (NCHEMS, 1994).

Once identified, these priorities can be attended to by a variety of budgetary mechanisms, each of which has particular strengths and weaknesses (Folger and Jones, 1993; Berdahl and Holland, 1989). Block grants, by which all eligible institutions are given resources up front in order to fund local activities consistent with statewide goals, appear most effective when the priorities funded are already congruent with what institutional leaders want to accomplish. Ohio's Selective Excellence program (NCHEMS, 1992a) and New Jersey's Governor's Challenge Grant (Berdahl and Holland, 1989) programs—both of mid-1980s vintage—provide informative examples of this approach. But experience has shown that such mechanisms have relatively little leverage in altering institutional behaviors more fundamentally where statewide goals do not match those of institutional leaders. Competitive grants like Colorado's Program Excellence awards or Oregon's Productivity Enhancement minigrants, in which institutions submit proposals in response to specific requests, excel at stimulating innovative ideas and are already consistent with research-oriented entrepreneurial cultures. But these are generally short term in nature and therefore tend to induce institutions to isolate specially funded from mainstream activities. Performance funds, which institutions are rewarded after the fact for demonstrated increases in performance generally measured quantitatively, are, like all formula-budgeting mechanisms, capable of exerting considerable leverage on institutional behavior. Tennessee's long-standing Instructional Evaluation Schedule provides the clearest instance (Banta, 1986), though perhaps the most striking current example is Funding for Results in Missouri (Stein, 1996). But such approaches require clear metrics for measuring performance and may encourage institutions to focus on ways of counting more than on actually changing underlying behaviors.

Given this array of strengths and weaknesses, experience has shown that these mechanisms are best used in combination to create effective markets for improvement. Most successful are comprehensive approaches that integrate the identification of clear priorities through strategic planning with a variety of specific categorical and incentive-based mechanisms each designed to make a market for a particular client or set of purposes. Again, Ohio's Selective Excellence approach provides a noteworthy example of how such a multi-faceted program might be configured (NCHEMS, 1992a). Also needed are assessment/accountability mechanisms that are able to track clearly the degree to which these investments are actually paying off. Other lessons about the use of such fiscal instruments, whether singly or in combination, include the following:

— keeping such incentives in place both in good times and bad; without a clear commitment to incentive funds as permanent components of the budget, institutions will be understandably reluctant to make basic changes to accommodate them (Jones, 1995).

— creating incentive pools that are large enough to command more than passing faculty and administrative attention; addition-to-base allocation mechanisms are now typically set at 1 to 5 percent of budget, while recent state experience demonstrates that perhaps twice to three times this component is required to cause real shifts in institutional behavior (NCHEMS, 1992a; Albright, 1996).

— keeping manageable the number of initiatives which create such markets. On the one hand, clear signals about the kinds of behaviors expected are required. On the other, the overhead associated with running large numbers of special purpose funding programs can quickly become overwhelming.

The deliberate use of state-level resource allocation mechanisms to affect fundamental changes in institutional operating environments is still in its infancy, but it is clearly on the rise. Some five states (Tennessee, Kentucky, Missouri, Arkansas, and South Carolina) now operate formal performance-budgeting systems, with an additional ten to twelve using other addition-to-base categorical methods to consciously redirect resources consistent with public purposes (Ewell, 1996). As already noted, the most promising appear to be those that directly fund clients or that consciously foster partnerships both between institutions and with other social actors (Albright and Gilleland, 1994). This is largely because such approaches embed accountability for results directly into the reward structure itself, the hallmark of a properly functioning market.

REMAKING THE STRUCTURE OF ACADEMIC ACCOUNTING

A major complement to the incentive structure provided by current resource allocation mechanisms is the credit-based coinage in terms of which academic activity is publicly accounted. Though its origins are voluntary, this system as well is a creature of public policy. While the original purpose of the Carnegie unit was to standardize course-based activities in order to facilitate student movement across institutions (and to a lesser extent, to establish quality controls by prescribing the minimum lengths of subject matter exposure in particular disciplines), it really proved indispensable in helping to determine costs. Together with its clock-hour variants, the credit hour also provided a critical definitional foundation for the federal student aid system, which constituted a major component of the fiscal incentive structure for both private and public institutions. Resource allocation mechanisms constructed in this manner produce powerful incentives for particular types of behavior. Less visible, but in many ways more pervasive, are the effects of the accounting mechanism itself.

One important impact of the credit system is the way it encourages the fragmentation of instructional experiences. Less apparent in traditional academic settings, this impact becomes decisive in the situation faced by most current students: distribution-based curricula, a wide choice of courses that meet requirements, and little advice about which choices to make. To the extent that credit-based public resource allocation mechanisms are replicated within institutions to provide funds to departments a further unintended effect is to encourage instructional isolation among teaching units. Probably the strongest consequences here are at institutions like Indiana University or the University of Southern California that have adopted recently fashionable Responsibility-Centered Management (RCM) approaches. In such cases, departments or schools compete freely in an attempt to maximize credit hours, with consequent damage to joint products like general education.

A second important impact of this form of accounting is its subtle reinforcement of the traditional production function of instruction. Overwhelmingly based on fixed-length classes in which all students learn the same things at the same time, the only way to boost learning productivity within this rubric is through increased economies of scale (Johnstone, 1993). Some of the most promising alternatives for breaking this mold, including time-independent learning in which students can proceed at their own pace (made far easier recently through the use of technology), and variable-length classes in which instructional time is adjusted to fit particular learning outcomes, have proven difficult to accommodate within a structure of academic accounting based essentially on length of exposure. A persistent finding across campuses uncovered in recent evaluations of technology-based courses in Oregon and Virginia, for instance, is the problem of determining appropriate faculty teaching loads under such circumstances (NCHEMS, 1996).

A final important difficulty with the current accounting structure is that it makes it hard to officially recognize and account for learning milestones between the individual course and the degree. Given escalating levels of multiinstitutional enrollment, as well as increasing numbers of students who step out of academic careers to enter the workforce without completing formal degree requirements, there is a growing need to formally recognize intermediate achievements for purposes of certification or transfer. Such milestones include specific sequences of courses or learning experiences that result in a particular body of job-related skills, or particular sets of general education abilities like applied mathematics. Intermediate certifications of this kind are rapidly becoming the coin of the realm in industry-provided workforce training (Drake Prometric, 1995) and provide promising alternatives to current course-by-course articulation structures among public colleges and universities.

The assessment initiatives launched by many states in the mid-to-late 1980s represent an early set of policy actions designed to reverse these tendencies. By 1990, some two-thirds of the states and all six regional accrediting bodies had adopted such programs, which essentially mandated institutions to define clear programmatic outcomes for instructional programs and assure that students were meeting them (Ewell, 1993). But although they call needed attention to accounting for the outputs of instructional activity, such initiatives can do little by themselves to alter underlying institutional economies based on time spent rather than products delivered. Coupled with marginal incentive programs, however, accounting outcomes can exert greater leverage. A simple, though effective, example is providing capstone payments to institutions for degrees produced, in addition to credit-based allocation, a mechanism which provides a built-in incentive for institutions to devote resources to student retention (Jones, 1995). New York's capitation-based Bundy Funds, available to private as well as public institutions for several decades, and Missouri's Funding for Results program provide useful illustrations of this approach. Performance funding schemes that link dollars with learning outcomes assessed directly through testing have proven more problematic, largely because the methods used are far less clear-cut and credible (Banta, 1986). If less ambiguous and controversial measures are used in such schemes (e.g. graduate placement or percent completing programs), and especially when institutions themselves have a hand in negotiating these measures to fit their own missions, as in Missouri, the effects on institutional behavior can become more apparent (Stein, 1996).

Recent attempts to remake the structure of academic accounting through state-level policy result finally from continuing escalation of the problem that the Carnegie-unit system was originally designed to address—transfer between educational units and sectors. One manifestation is growing state interest in establishing competency-based admissions requirements for public colleges and universities (SHEEO, 1989). Pilot programs founded on this concept are now deployed or contemplated in about a half-dozen states, including most prominently Oregon, Wisconsin, and Florida. In these and other states, the logic of this approach is also being extended to the vexing problem of interinstitutional transfer within the postsecondary sector. A more fundamental stimulus for remaking the credit-based system is the growing salience of alternative modes of instruction, especially asynchronous distance delivery through such media as the Internet. Under such circumstances, time-based units of instructional activity become entirely irrelevant, placing the appropriate focus of academic accounting solely on the outcome or credential. One salutary effect of such radical attempts to remake the system as the recently announced western virtual university (Western Governors Association [WGA], 1996), coupled with an expanding network of industry certifications of technical skills, is that they do exactly that.

Experience with alternative methods for accounting academic work at the state level is far less extensive than that associated with directed budgeting. Nevertheless, some important guidelines for their further development can also be put forward:

1. The message behind any measure of output used as a substitute for seat-time should be made clear to the academic units affected. In the short term, metrics based on concrete outputs (like degrees completed, or numbers of previously deficient students successfully attaining college-level status) may be more effective than those founded on complex assessments of student learning, if only because they signal more clearly what is wanted and avoid the substantial methodological debates typically involved in assessing outcomes directly.

2. Establishing such measures should be preceded by extensive prior discussion and consensus building to promote real understanding of these implied messages within the institutional community, and the measures chosen should credibly certify attainment for external audiences. This is especially important for any alternative credentialing approach. Current best practice in competency-based curricula in K–12 settings, for example, as well as technical certifica-

tion in industry, requires disclosure of both the fact of attainment and the specific types of demonstrations actually used to certify it (New Standards, 1996).

3. These measures should be constructed in such a way that they can be positively influenced by the right kinds of institutional action. Alternative measures of academic activity and impact require safeguards against institutions acting only to manage the numbers. Rewarding institutions for successful program completion rates, for example, may obscure the fact that such rates are largely attained by lowered standards or greater up-front selectivity. As a result, any such alternatives must be used in combination, with checks and balances between measures designed in from the beginning to ensure that such abuses do not occur.

Supplementing long-established seat-time measures with more appropriate and flexible methods for accounting academic activity and achievement at the state level will undoubtedly be a long process. At the same time, credit-based systems will remain appropriate for many state-level management functions such as examining long-term changes in the demand for instruction in particular fields, or changes in student course-taking behavior. But breaking the current dominance of such mechanisms in state-level cost accounting and their consequent impacts on institutional incentive structures will ultimately be critical in creating markets for instructional innovation.

REMAKING ACCOUNTABILITY AND QUALITY ASSURANCE

The current array of external accountability and quality-assurance mechanisms affecting colleges and universities was also established in an era of institutional activity quite different from today's. State-level accountability began primarily with fiscal oversight, often in considerable detail, until most public universities gained large measures of fiscal autonomy in the 1960s and 1970s. More recently, as public complaints about higher education's performance have risen, state-level accountability has broadened to include other aspects of institutional behavior. At the same time, traditional accountability and quality-assurance functions continue to be discharged (though with diminishing public credibility) by voluntary accrediting bodies.

Since 1990, discussions about the structure, alignment, and need for such functions have increased in prominence. On the one hand, public officials have made it clear that higher education, like other public enterprises, must become much more visibly accountable for performance. On the other hand, many in government and virtually all academics think that current approaches to accountability are both unwieldy and ineffective. But the history of this topic over the past five years has been one of uncertainty and vacillation. Unprecedented federal attempts to increase institutional oversight in the light of the perceived failures of accreditation in 1989–94 (including most prominently the short-lived State Postsecondary Review Program) were succeeded quickly by a hands-off attitude in the wake of the 1994 elections. Early attempts to remake accreditation on a more comprehensive national basis and align it with public purposes under the banner of the National Policy Board (NPB) on institutional accreditation suffered a similar fate when strong opposition from private institutions arose (Ewell and Wellman, 1996). Yet demands for greater accountability continue unabated. The current national dilemma with regard to quality assurance, put succinctly, is that there is no political support for achieving accountability through centralized means, but there also remains no real conception of what an appropriate system of accountability other than government control ought to look like.

Part of the problem is that the motives for establishing and operating such mechanisms have never been clear. Institutional accreditation, for example, has always sought to incorporate within a single process the very different functions of guaranteeing quality based on minimum standards, and of providing a stimulus for institutional self-improvement. But growing criticism of voluntary accreditation is based in large part on its inability to do both effectively. State-based assessment initiatives launched throughout the 1980s were intended to be similarly multifunctional. Most also proved deficient in providing real accountability, and were supplemented quickly in many states with performance-indicator systems that involved direct institutional comparisons (Ruppert, 1994).

Remaking structures of accountability and quality assurance to be more supportive of high performance thus requires a clarification of what such mechanisms are really attempting to accomplish. Embedded within most current accountability mechanisms—whether governmental or voluntary—for example, are at least four distinct functions:

1. General public accountability. This purpose embraces both direct accountability for the expenditure of public funds and the overall returns on investment associated with these funds. While it need not involve explicit comparisons between institutions, the process should minimally allow summative judgments to be made about cost-effectiveness and the current condition of the asset in ways that communicate directly to a lay audience. A parallel accountability mechanism outside higher education might be a corporate stockholders' report.

2. Assuring capacity. This purpose centers on determining whether or not a given institution is minimally capable of doing what it claims to do. Basic consumer protection falls within this rubric, together with a range of contractual relationships between institutions and employers or other external bodies. The information required in this case must be directly accessible to the clients involved, but oriented toward an institution's ability to meet specific minimum standards of interest to these clients. Relevant parallels would include compliance with building codes, the certification of products by scientific laboratories, or independent bond rating.

3. Informing choice. This purpose centers on providing information that will enable higher education's various customers to make individual purchasing decisions. This demands comparative information on a set of performance dimensions of specific interest to particular clients. A parallel might be the product reviews contained in *Consumer Reports.*

4. Recommending internal improvement. This purpose centers explicitly on providing direct guidance about what needs to be done. Such information needs to be in considerable detail, but should emphatically not be public because, without knowledge about context and intended remedial actions, it will likely be misinterpreted. A parallel mechanism outside higher education might be a consulting report or the management letter accompanying the results of a financial audit.

Many of the same pieces of information are relevant across all four of these purposes—for example, the number and proportion of students graduating from an institution's programs or the number of graduates obtaining employment in a field related to the training they received. But the ways in which data are presented, the extent to which they are shared, and the manner in which they are used may vary significantly.

Dissecting these quite different purposes is also important because it highlights the ways in which individual accountability mechanisms must work together to deliberately shape the behaviors of institutions. Market-based systems that capitalize on consumer information, for example, are now fashionable because they are consistent with the rhetoric of deregulation, because they appear to best fit the diverse universe of current higher education providers, and because they can respond flexibly to the quite different needs of different quality-assurance constituencies including potential students, employers, and public officials. But the market may be far more effective in influencing behavior in some sectors than in others, and may be extremely uneven in assuring quality on particular dimensions of interest. For these reasons, the appropriate use of regulatory and direct incentive mechanisms becomes important—not to replace the operation of the market, but to actively shape it in particular directions. Following this logic, state-level action can first be used to ensure that basic consumer information is present (ECS, 1995). Incentive funding, in turn, can be directed toward meeting particular state-level objectives, with accountability for results built into the incentive mechanism itself. An approach that consciously orchestrates these strategies as part of a distributed system of quality assurance appears far more promising than purely regulatory or market-driven alternatives (Ewell and Wellman, 1996).

Establishing such a distributed system of quality assurance on a national basis requires a clear division of labor between current accountability players, including federal and state agencies, as well as institutional and program accreditors. While rejecting current approaches that apply the same standards to all providers under all circumstances, it must be constructed to recognize that the various quality-assurance mechanisms operated by particular external actors and agencies in their own interests have legitimately different purposes and clients, and may thus employ quite different processes and standards. Assuring the integration and coherence of such a system, in turn, requires considerable information-sharing between these parties at interest. As has already been demonstrated in such areas as health care, the role of the federal government is in this regard especially salient, particularly in the realm of establishing common definitions of key data elements and the creation of databases that all parties can use (Ewell, 1996).

Such an alternative to the current duplicative and prescriptive array of external quality assurance processes is only being talked about at this point. But experiences in both other public enterprises and in other nations suggest a number of important guidelines for further development. These include the following:

1. *Reduce reporting burdens.* Established reporting requirements associated with both government authorities and private agencies have grown significantly in the last two decades but in a piecemeal fashion and with unclear purposes. At the same time, traditional modes of reporting—most prominently, comprehensive narrative self-studies—have become both increasingly burdensome for institutions and programs to prepare, and are less and less helpful in actually discharging accountability. A promising recent development among both states and accreditors has therefore been to design alternatives that rely much more heavily on common statistical indicators and concrete exhibits related to institutional performance that are far less time-consuming to prepare and interpret (Ewell, 1996).

2. *Reduce duplication.* Improved information sharing founded on common definitions of key indicators and terms also allows better coordination of the many similar reports now produced by colleges and universities for various agencies, both private and governmental. Clearer divisions of labor between the different parties at interest would also help to address the growing burden of duplicative reporting. In the definitional arena, at least, there are some signs that this is beginning to occur (American Association of State Colleges and Universities, 1995).

3. *Capitalize on centralized databases and third-party data collectors.* Some two-thirds of the states are now engaged in operating or constructing comprehensive unit-record enrollment databases for their public higher education systems (Russell and Chisholm, 1995). Increasing use is also being made of other large-scale administrative databases such as state-level wage-record systems for constructing outcome measures automatically (Seppanen, 1995). In both cases, institutions appear ready to allow state authorities to obtain information directly in order to reduce reporting burdens, even though government access to it might potentially increase intrusiveness. Other

states are examining outsourcing such information-collection, where appropriate, for example in obtaining ratings of alumni and employer satisfaction (Ewell, 1996).

4. *Tailor reporting to specific audiences and purposes.* The general-purpose nature of current accountability-reporting mechanisms not only makes them burdensome, but it also obstructs the ability of different client groups to get useful answers to their particular questions. As a result, some states are deliberately reconstructing accountability reporting to explicitly reflect and respond to the information needs of these different constituencies.

5. *Reflect systemic as well as institutional perspectives.* The increasingly interdependent nature of the higher education enterprise also implies that accountability be founded as much on the achievement of collective as on unit-based objectives. Indeed, the majority of objectives related to public purposes—for example, access, affordability, or contributions to statewide economic development—make little sense if approached only in terms of institution-specific contributions. To continue to foster attention to such ends, and to ensure the kinds of interinstitutional cooperation required to attain them, more and better measures of system performance are needed.

Despite initial efforts consistent with these injunctions, the accountability dilemma remains vexing for all concerned. On the one hand, reducing institutional accountability burdens is considered essential to meet productivity demands. On the other hand, strong accountability mechanisms are needed to ensure that the resulting actions are consistent with established purposes. The promising answer for higher education increasingly appears to be one of abandoning accountability as reporting to those in an oversight role in favor of a view that stresses its role in providing information to a range of interested parties. Not only does the latter construction deemphasize compliance, it also emphasizes the need to make what is reported connect visibly with identifiable clients who have real decisions to make. Without such a reorientation, accountability functions can never act as more than a tax on the higher education enterprise—adding costs, but yielding little additional value for anyone involved.

The issues raised by this final section are in many ways familiar. Institutions routinely complain that a myriad of conflicting policies, regulations, and incentives inhibit their efforts to achieve higher levels of performance. As a result, they repeatedly claim that public authorities would obtain a better return on their higher education investments if they simply left colleges and universities alone. In part they are right, but relaxing compliance is only half of what is required. Without explicit direction and incentives, academic institutions have demonstrated that they are quite willing to pursue their own agendas. For most institutions, these continue to emphasize discipline-based, research-oriented priorities that provide maximum opportunities for faculty to enhance individual scholarly reputations. It is in this direction, after all, that their current reward structure lies—constructed for them, for the most part, by past policy decisions. Policies designed only to prevent them from pursuing such objectives are bound to fail without a larger vision of what society as a whole wants its higher education system to accomplish. Little such broad direction-setting has occurred in public forums of late, and it is badly needed. Achieving high performance in a responsive university will require leaders both on college campuses and in public arenas to be prepared to take on this task.

References

Ahumada, M. M. (1990). "An Analysis of State Formula Budgeting in Higher Education." In *Higher Education: Handbook of Theory and Research, VI*, ed. J. C. Smart. New York: Agathon Press, 467–97.

Albright, B. N. (1996). *From Business as Usual to Funding for Results*. Working paper prepared for the Ohio Higher Education Funding Commission. Columbus: Ohio Board of Regents.

Albright, B. N., and D. S. Gilleland. (1994). "A Clean Slate: Principles for Moving to a Value-Driven Higher Education Funding Model." In *Focus on the Budget: Rethinking Current Practice*, ed. R. M. Epper. Denver: State Higher Education Executive Officers (SHEEO) and Education Commission of the States (ECS), 7–22.

American Association of State Colleges and Universities (1995). *Report of the Joint Commission on Accountability Reporting*. Washington, D.C.: American Association of State Colleges and Universities (AASCU).

Banta, T. W. (1986). *Performance Funding in Higher Education: A Critical Analysis of Tennessee's Experience*. Boulder: National Center for Higher Education Management Systems.

Berdahl, R. O. and B. A. Holland, eds. (1989). *Developing Fiscal Incentives to Improve Higher Education: Proceedings from a National Invitation Conference*. College Park, Md: National Center for Postsecondary Governance and Finance.

Brinkman, P. T. (1984). "Formula Budgeting: The Fourth Decade." In *Responding to*

New Realities in Funding, New Directions for Institutional Research #43, ed. L. L. Leslie. San Francisco: Jossey-Bass, 21–34.

Drake Prometric (1995). *The Complete Guide to Certification for Computing Professionals*. New York: McGraw-Hill.

Eaton, J. S. (1992). "The Evolution of Access Policy: 1965–1990." *American Higher Education: Purposes, Problems, and Public Perspectives*. Queenstown, Md: The Aspen Institute, 141–58.

Education Commission of the States (1995). *Making Quality Count in Undergraduate Education*. Denver: Education Commission of the States (ECS).

Ewell, P. T. (1985). *Levers for Change: The Role of State Government in Improving the Quality of Postsecondary Education*. Denver: Education Commission of the States (ECS).

———. (1990). *Assessment and the "New Accountability": A Challenge for Higher Education's Leadership*. Denver: Education Commission of the States (ECS).

———. (1993). "The Role of States and Accreditors in Shaping Assessment Practice." In *Making a Difference: Outcomes of a Decade of Assessment in Higher Education*, eds. T. W. Banta and Associates. San Francisco: Jossey-Bass, 339–56.

———. (1994a). *Restoring Our Links with Society: The Neglected Art of Collective Responsibility*. Metropolitan Universities, Summer, 1994, 79–87.

———. (1994b). "A Matter of Integrity: Accountability and the Future of Self-Regulation." *Change*, 26(6): 24–29.

———. (1995). *Toward Common Ground: Defining and Assuring "Quality" in Undergraduate Education*. Working paper prepared for Governor Roy Romer's "Quality Counts" Agenda. Denver: Education Commission of the States (ECS).

———. (1996). *The National Assessment of College Student Learning: An Inventory of State-Level Assessment Activities: Report of the Third Study Design Workshop*. Washington, D.C.: National Center for Education Statistics (NCES), U.S. Department of Education.

Ewell, P. T. and J. Wellman. (1996). *Re-Fashioning Accountability Toward a "Distributed" System of Quality Assurance*. Working paper prepared for an Ad Hoc Study Group on Postsecondary Accountability. Denver: Education Commission of the States (ECS).

Folger, J. and D. P. Jones. (1993). *Using Fiscal Policy to Achieve State Education Goals: State Policy and Collegiate Learning*. Denver: Education Commission of the States (ECS).

Gardiner, L. F. (1994). *Redesigning Higher Education: Producing Dramatic Gains in Student Learning*. Report #7, ASHE-ERIC Higher Education Reports. Washington, D.C.: George Washington University.

Johnstone, D. B. (1993). "Learning Productivity: A New Imperative for American Higher Education." *Studies in Public Higher Education*, State University of New York (SUNY), 3, April, 1–33.

Jones, D. P. (1984). *Higher Education Budgeting at the State Level: Concepts and Principles*. Boulder: National Center for Higher Education Management Systems (NCHEMS).

———. (1995). *Strategic Budgeting: The Board's Role in Public Colleges and Universities*.

AGB Occasional Paper #28. Washington, D.C.: Association of Governing Boards of Universities and Colleges.

Jones, D. P. and P. T. Ewell. (1993). *The Effect of State Policy on Undergraduate Education: State Policy and Collegiate Learning.* Denver: Education Commission of the States (ECS).

Keppel, F. (1991). "The Role of Public Policy in Higher Education in the United States: Land Grants to Pell Grants and Beyond." In *The Uneasy Public Policy Triangle in Higher Education: Quality, Diversity, and Budgetary Efficiency,* D. H. Finifter, R. G. Baldwin, and J. R. Thelin, eds. New York: ACE / Macmillan, 9–17.

Levine, A. (1978). *Handbook on Undergraduate Curriculum, A Report for the Carnegie Council on Policy Studies in Higher Education.* San Francisco: Jossey-Bass.

McGuinness, A. C., Jr. (1994a). "The Changing Structure of State Higher Education Leadership." In *State Postsecondary Education Structures Handbook: State Coordinating and Governing Boards,* eds. A. C. McGuinness, Jr., R. Epper, and S. Arredondo. Denver: Education Commission of the States (ECS), 1–45.

———. (1994b). *A Framework for Evaluating State Policy Roles in Improving Undergraduate Education: Stimulating Long-Term Systemic Change.* Denver: Education Commission of the States (ECS).

———. (1996). "A Model for Successful Restructuring." In *Restructuring Higher Education: What Works and What Doesn't in Reorganizing Governing Systems,* ed. T. J. McTaggart and Associates. San Francisco: Jossey-Bass, 203–29.

McTaggart, T. J., and Associates (1996). *Restructuring Higher Education: What Works and What Doesn't in Reorganizing Governing Systems.* San Francisco: Jossey-Bass.

National Center for Higher Education Management Systems (1992a). *An Evaluation of the Ohio Selective Excellence Program.* Boulder: National Center for Higher Education Management Systems (NCHEMS).

———. (1992b). "Higher Education Finance: Back to Basics." *NCHEMS Newsletter,* 5, September.

———. (1994). "Designing State Policy for a New Higher Education Environment." *NCHEMS Newsletter,* 10, October.

———. (1996). "The Promise of Technology-Based Instruction: What We Are Learning." *NCHEMS News,* 13, March.

Newman, F. (1987). *Choosing Quality: Reducing Conflict Between the State and the University.* Denver: Education Commission of the States (ECS).

New Standards (1996). *Performance Standards: Consultation Draft.* Pittsburgh: National Center on Education and the Economy.

Osborne, D. and T. Gaebler. (1992). *Reinventing Government: How the Entrepreneurial Spirit is Transforming the Public Sector.* Reading, Mass.: Addison-Wesley.

Parsons, T. and G. M. Platt. (1973). *The American University.* Cambridge: Harvard University Press.

Perkin, H. (1984). "The Historical Perspective." In *Perspectives on Higher Education: Eight Disciplinary and Comparative Views,* ed. B. R. Clark. Berkeley: University of California Press, 17–55.

Pew Higher Education Research Program (1990). "The Lattice and the Ratchet." *Policy Perspectives,* 2(4): 1–8.

Richardson, W. C. (1996). "A Peacetime Mission for Higher Education." *Trusteeship* 4(4): 36.

Rudolph, F. (1977). *Curriculum: A History of the American Undergraduate Course of Study Since 1636.* San Francisco: Jossey-Bass.

Ruppert, S. S. (1996). *The Politics of Remedy: State Legislative Views on Higher Education.* Washington, D.C.: National Education Association (NEA).

Ruppert, S. S., ed. (1994). *Charting Higher Education Accountability: A Sourcebook on State-Level Performance Indicators.* Denver: Education Commission of the States (ECS).

Russell, A. B. and M. P. Chisholm. (1995). "Tracking in Multi-Institutional Contexts." In *Student Tracking: New Techniques, New Demands,* New Directions for Institutional Research #87, ed. P. T. Ewell. San Francisco: Jossey-Bass, 43–54.

Seppanen, L. J. (1995). "Linkages to the World of Employment." In *Student Tracking: New Techniques, New Demands,* New Directions for Institutional Research #87, ed. P. T. Ewell. San Francisco: Jossey-Bass, 77–92.

State Higher Education Executive Officers (1989). *New Issues—New Roles: A Conversation with State Higher Education Executive Officers.* Denver: Education Commission of the States (ECS) and State Higher Education Executive Officers (SHEEO).

Stein, R. B. (1996). "Performance Reporting / Funding Program: Missouri's Efforts to Integrate State and Campus Strategic Planning." In *Performance Indicators in Higher Education: What Works, What Doesn't, and What's Next?* Proceedings of a Pre-Conference Symposium for the 11th AAHE Conference on Assessment and Quality. College Station: Texas A&M University System, 36–58.

Western Governors Association (1996). *From Vision to Reality: The Western Virtual University.* Denver: Western Governors' Association (WGA).

The Responsive University
in the Twenty-first Century

KENT M. KEITH

🎓 🎓 🎓

WHEN I WAS THE PRESIDENT OF A SMALL PRIVATE UNIVERSITY IN THE LATE 1980s and early 1990s, one of my most important functions was to challenge our institution's assumptions about what we did and why we did it. We knew that significant changes were occurring in student demographics, recruitment and financial aid practices, student demand for certain subjects, the cost of money, the actions of competing institutions, government policies, and the focus of accreditation. We knew that we needed to respond to these changes. And yet, when we tried to respond, we often found ourselves boxed in by old assumptions.

This book is about getting out of the box. It is about rethinking fundamental assumptions of higher education—assumptions that worked in the late twentieth century but can trap and immobilize our institutions in the twenty-first century. The fundamental assumptions examined in this book include the concepts of service to students and society, tenure, internal decision making, government policy, and institutional accountability. The treatment of these issues is both innovative and practical: innovative because the authors point us in new directions; practical because the new directions build on the current functions and cultures of our institutions. The authors point to a new kind of institution of higher education—the "responsive" college or university. The purpose of this chapter is to bring together their suggestions and observations by painting a composite picture of what the responsive college or university will look like.

The Need for Responsive Institutions

The need to develop responsive colleges and universities in the United States was established more than 130 years ago. Rudolph (1962) estimated that more than seven hundred colleges died in the United States before 1860. Two major explanations may account for their relatively short lives: (1) there was not enough money to support all of the nation's colleges, and (2) most of the colleges no longer responded to the needs of those they purported to serve.

We are not likely to see the demise of seven hundred institutions in the coming decades, but we will see major changes, and for the same two reasons. First, there is not enough money to support all our institutions of higher education in the manner to which they have become accustomed. Second, many of those who control the funding of higher education do not believe that our colleges and universities are responsive to the needs of students or society at large.

Roger Benjamin and Steve Carroll outline the financial picture in Chapter Four. The costs of providing higher education are outstripping inflation, and there are growing demands for service. In the foreseeable future, however, real public revenues per student are likely to face slow growth, possibly even outright decline. Public resistance to tuition increases at private institutions is also noticeable. Money will continue to be in short supply.

In Chapter Five, Peter Ewell describes the crisis of confidence in the ability of colleges and universities to respond appropriately to public needs and concerns. He notes that public officials who see a fundamental lack of responsiveness in academic institutions may be willing to turn their backs on them. This can lead to even fewer resources.

To survive and thrive, colleges and universities will have to be responsive. Responsiveness is in the eyes of those being served: students, parents, governments, businesses, nonprofit organizations. Each of these publics will judge the university in terms of the quality of their relationships with the university, and the quality of the outcomes of those relationships.

To be responsive, institutions of higher education will need to be service oriented. They will need new internal relationships, including relationships between faculty members which support planning and evaluation processes, and relationships between faculty and administrators which support lateral decision-making structures. Responsive colleges and universities will also need new external relationships, including social partnerships with the communities and regions they serve, partnerships with government policy makers, and joint ventures with other institutions. Higher education will need to focus on outcomes, and the outcomes produced must be relevant to the needs of those who live beyond the campus walls. Finally, responsive institutions will take advantage of alternative instructional methods that can deliver quality outcomes, and they will establish extensive communications networks and dispersed teaching sites throughout the communities and regions they serve.

Service-Oriented Institutions

As Ellen Chaffee argues in Chapter One, colleges and universities must focus on customers, listen to their needs and desires, and serve them in appropriate ways. This service orientation includes the ability to think through problems and issues from the customer's point of view. For whose convenience is the current system designed? If it is not designed for the convenience of those served, it will need to be redesigned.

The word *customer* may sound overly commercial to members of academe. However, the word calls our attention to the constituents we serve and reminds us that we need to meet their needs and expectations if we are to succeed. We will need to be student centered in our undergraduate programs, community centered in our outreach programs, and nation centered in our research activities.

A true service orientation toward students will have an impact on teaching. The focus will shift from how faculty members teach to how students learn. Learning methods will become diversified. There will be peer study groups, small group interactions with faculty, traditional lectures, simulations, interactive software, and extensive use of information resources including the Internet (Guskin, 1994). The faculty role will be more complex and will include lecturing, facilitating, coaching, and designing customized learning experiences, in order to stimulate student learning.

A service orientation does not mean abandoning the search for truth and the advancement of knowledge. We will still seek to discover and disseminate truth. However, if our colleges and universities are responsive, the truths we discover and disseminate will be relevant; they will change lives. It is when the activities of our colleges and universities are aligned with the highest priority needs of society that we will have the greatest positive impact.

Internal Relationships

The ability of our colleges and universities to become responsive will depend first on internal relationships. Faculty members are the key resource. A college or university will not be responsive unless its members of faculty are responsive. And faculty responsiveness is not something that the administration can mandate. Faculty members are hired to be independent professionals performing the same basic tasks throughout their careers. The direct, daily supervision of faculty by the administration is not feasible because administrators cannot be in every classroom, and even if they were, they would not know enough about each specialty to adequately supervise instruction. Also, highly detailed lists of job duties imposed by administrators are likely to backfire (Levin, 1991). Meanwhile, the tenure system can be seen as an obstacle to change, since it protects faculty who may be doing a good job but not the job that most needs to be done.

In Chapter Two, William Tierney suggests that we look past the argument over tenure and seek ways to encourage faculty members to set and meet goals for their own performance. Faculty members will respond to new opportunities and needs if they support each other in continuous personal and professional planning and assessment. This planning and assessment will not only result in professional growth and improved productivity but will also allow members of faculty to regularly review and take into account shifts in student demand, resource allocations, departmental goals, and the evolving mission of the institution.

The performance contract, which defines a faculty member's goals for the year, is a planning tool with immense potential. Faculty goals can take into consideration not only the interests and plans of the faculty member, but also the goals of the department and the mission of the institution in responding to the needs of students and the larger society. Discussion of faculty goals will stimulate annual reconsideration of the underlying assumptions and will allow individuals and departments to plan step-by-step changes which are coordinated with other faculty members and departments.

Faculty performance contracts can thus determine, one by one, both the extent to which, and the ways in which, the institution will be a responsive college or university. Without annual faculty goals, it will be nearly impossible to move in new directions that respond to the needs of students and society. When faculty members do have individual goals, they can be supported in achieving their goals, for their own benefit as well as that of the institution and those it serves.

This continuous planning and assessment will require new faculty relationships, built on a sense of the obligations that faculty have to each other. The bases for change described by Tierney include a climate of encouragement, formative assessment discussions between faculty and department chairs or deans, and the acceptance of assessment and evaluation as an ongoing, core activity of the academic community. Tenure remains but is embedded in a new culture typified by an increase in input, advice, and support between faculty, as well as greater dialogue with administrators.

Individual faculty performance goals will link into the new structure of decision making which Benjamin and Carroll describe in Chapter Four. There are not enough resources to allow individual faculty members and their departments to make decisions without weighing the impacts on the institution. At the same time, the leaders of the institution are not experts in each of the disciplines or activities that must be analyzed and compared to make effective decisions. A horizontal or lateral information-sharing system can bring faculty and administration together to look at the parts and their relation to the whole. In doing so, the institutional mission, departmental goals, and individual faculty goals will influence each other. This ongoing, iterative decision-making process will require new relationships between faculty and administrators. The quality of those relationships will depend not only on information but on a high level of mutual trust.

Establishing a new structure for decision making will not be easy. Weick (1976) described schools as loosely coupled systems. The decentralized units in a loosely coupled system are quick to pick up trends and ideas, and can respond effectively to their specific constituencies. However, when the entire organization needs to make decisions which affect all its parts, especially in a crisis, tightly coupled systems are more effective. Because the organizational cultures of universities do not accept tightly coupled systems, Benjamin and Carroll describe a system which is somewhere between tight and loose and recognizes both the decentralized culture and the crisis which requires organization-wide decisions. The system they propose could be described as "information coupled."

External Relationships

The responsive college or university will not only have new internal relationships, but new external relationships as well. In Chapter Three, Larry Braskamp and Jon Wergin provide concrete examples of a university's responsiveness in serving the common good. They describe the challenges faced by faculty members in developing quality relationships with members of the community when working together with them in the field to solve problems or make improvements. A quality relationship is one in which each member of the team has a contribution to make, and the contributions are complementary. This is not something that can be unilaterally determined from the campus. Faculty members and administrators must identify issues, listen to others, and define the roles that make the best use of what the university has to offer. Not every need can be met. Quality relationships, characterized by mutuality and equality, will provide universities with the information and insight they will need to make informed choices.

In Chapter Five, Peter Ewell describes the challenges in clarifying and articulating relationships with external bodies, especially state government policy makers. Universities need clear signals from the government regarding its priorities, because there will only be enough resources to meet high priority needs. Ewell suggests that partnerships with government will be necessary to transform institutional performance so that it is better aligned with public purposes.

Ewell also suggests joint ventures across academic units and between institutions—partnerships which could reduce duplication and enhance quality. Incentives should be provided for joint ventures which include not only colleges and universities but also schools, libraries, corporations, and government agencies.

As with internal decision making, the development of new relationships with government leaders and organizations will require trust. However, thoughtfully designed and effective political relationships can produce the combination of coherent public policy and institutional flexibility that will be essential to success.

New Conversations

The responsive university will be closely connected with many publics, and will be in constant conversation with them. The conversations which take place in new social partnerships will be different from those most faculty engage in at present. Faculty members who have been socialized and trained into the values, methods, and norms of their academic disciplines and are accustomed to focusing on discourse with others in their specialized fields will have new behaviors and "languages" to learn. A major task will be the translation of academic knowledge into forms that are usable for nonacademics, and the conversion of nonacademic knowledge into forms that are usable for academics.

The conversations which take place in government partnerships and institutional joint ventures will be different from those most administrators engage in at present. Administrators who have focused on obtaining resources and other advantages for their own institutions will find it necessary to think in terms of system-wide policies, regional benefits, joint ventures, and the contributions of other types of institutions as well as their own in meeting a variety of public needs.

Direct involvement in social partnerships is messy, as Braskamp and Wergin remind us. Direct involvement in partnerships with government and other institutions is complicated, as Ewell points out. However, knowledge and experience will flow in both directions, enriching the partners as well as those served. The potential rewards to individuals, universities, and society are significant.

Emphasis on Outcomes

Responsiveness will not only depend on quality relationships, but also on the quality of the *outcomes* of those relationships. The responsive university has to deliver the right results.

Few people off-campus believe that a university is self-justifying. The justification is in the outcomes—relevant, high-quality education, research, and service. By discovering truth and using knowledge to meet people's needs, the responsive university can make a moral claim to the necessary resources. These resources will not be for the university, but for those who are served by the university. As colleges and universities stand alongside other institutions and agencies asking for money and support, the university must be able to argue, credibly, that it is making a unique, relevant, high-quality contribution to the people of its community and region.

The general public is not certain that universities currently provide the right outcomes. Two-thirds of the state governments now require some form of institutional assessment for institutions of higher education. All six regional accrediting agencies have policies requiring colleges and universities to assess their effectiveness. The Western Association of Schools and Colleges (WASC) calls for "a culture of evidence"—that is, an institutional culture which constantly seeks evidence of its effectiveness (1992: 2).

In the past, accrediting agencies have focused on measuring *inputs*—the number of library books, the number of Ph.D.s on the faculty, the number of dollars in the bank, the quality of facilities. WASC has been engaged in serious discussions with its member institutions about shifting to the measurement of *outcomes*—what students are learning. This is harder to measure, but there is a professional and even a moral obligation to try to measure it. Are we adding value? Are we making a difference? If we are making a difference, is it the difference that we and others want us to be making? We need to know.

Knowing will be difficult. The assessment of learning is complex, requiring a series of measurements and professional judgments. No doubt, multiple sources of evidence should be used wherever possible. A grade from a single faculty member or assessor does not tell us enough. Student achievement portfolios can include entrance and exit examinations, essays, research projects, exhibits, examination results in each course, and results on standard national tests such as the Graduate Record Exam. Teaching effectiveness must be assessed; alumni satisfaction should be surveyed.

The shift to an emphasis on outcomes will allow us to rethink our assumptions about what Ewell calls the traditional "production function" of instruction. Fixed-length classes, with a set number of hours of "seat time," will no longer be the key form of academic accounting. Academic accounting will not be concerned with the time spent, but with the learning outcomes that are delivered. This opens the door to the possibility of time-independent learning, with students proceeding at their own pace; variable-length classes that are tailored to specific learning outcomes; and distance learning through media such as the Internet. If these alternative methods result in student learning outcomes that are equal to or higher in quality than traditional methods, the responsive college and university will have an array of new tools to use in meeting the needs of their students.

Beyond the Campus Walls

Because of the emphasis on relationships and outcomes, the responsive college and university of the twenty-first century will be more a network than a place. The network will support the institution's relationships and provide constant feedback on needs and results. Successful institutions of higher education will thus be characterized by extensive communications systems and dispersed teaching and research sites which are closer to the publics being served.

Most early American colleges sought a degree of detachment from the surrounding community. The old-time "college on the hill" literally looked down on others. (At Harvard, which is very definitely *not* located on a hilltop, students still speak of "coming up" when they matriculate and "going down" when they graduate.) Braskamp and Wergin mention the gates, walls, and trees which buffer the campus from the outside world. Such barriers send the unfriendly signal that the college or university prefers to be isolated, physically and psychologically.

As campuses were built in the United States in the twentieth century, many universities became cities unto themselves. The bigger they became, the more urban responsibilities they assumed, constructing and maintaining their own roads, water, sewage, drainage, electric power backup, residence halls, meeting halls, office buildings, food service, recreational facilities, athletic fields, theaters, and health services. These university functions duplicated many of the services available in the cities and towns in which they were located.

More recently, colleges and universities have established continuing education programs and degree-completion programs which are taught at off-campus centers convenient to older students. Entrepreneurial and open universities have also grown, using a variety of delivery systems including printed materials, videos, satellite TV, teleconferencing, interactive software, and e-mail. These delivery systems bring the university to the student, instead of requiring the student to go to the university.

In the twenty-first century, responsive colleges and universities will adopt many of these new delivery systems to extend their networks and services beyond their campus walls. They will thus become decentralized, with offices and activities located throughout the communities and regions they serve. The main campus of today will become a major node in a dispersed system which supports the institution's external relations and provides direct services to a variety of publics.

Conclusion

Change takes time, and even when change arrives, it does not affect everyone. The authors of this book do not predict an overnight transformation. The core functions of the college and university, and many of their patterns of behavior, will remain.

However, the responsive university will be a different kind of university from what is common today. It will have new internal faculty relationships which support planning and assessment, and new lateral information-coupled decision-making structures. It will be closely connected to its publics, listening and responding to high-priority needs. Faculty members will have new external relationships with people in their communities and regions; administrators will have new external relationships with government agencies as well as schools, libraries, corporations, and other colleges and universities. Faculty members of the responsive university will participate in social partnerships which will force them to grapple with new kinds of knowledge and produce new kinds of truth. The administrators of the responsive university will participate in government partnerships and joint ventures which will force them to see beyond their own campuses to the common good of the larger community.

The responsive college and university will be focused on serving others. In serving others well, the university will enhance its contribution to students and society, and will attract the resources needed to continue its work. In establishing social and governmental partnerships, the faculty and administration will find fulfillment in engaging in the richness of the human condition and influencing the future of the human enterprise.

References

Guskin, A. (1994). "Reducing Student Costs and Enhancing Student Learning Part II: Restructuring the Role of Faculty." *Change* 26(5): 16–25.

Levin, H. (1991). "Raising Productivity in Higher Education." *Journal of Higher Education* 62(3): 241–62.

Rudolph, F. (1990). *The American College and University*. 1962. Reprint. Athens: University of Georgia Press.

Weick, K. (1976). "Educational Organizations as Loosely Coupled Systems." *Administrative Science Quarterly* 21(1): 1–19.

Western Association of Schools and Colleges. (1992). *Achieving Instutional Effectiveness Through Assessment: A Resource Manual to Support WASC Institutions*. Oakland, Calif.: Western Association of Schools and Colleges.

CONTRIBUTORS

ROGER BENJAMIN is director of the Institute on Education and Training at the RAND Corporation and a former provost at the University of Pittsburgh and the University of Minnesota.

LARRY A. BRASKAMP has been executive director of the Council for Higher Education and a former dean of the College of Education at the University of Illinois in Chicago.

STEVE CARROLL is senior economist at RAND and former deputy director of the Institute of Civil Justice, RAND.

ELLEN EARLE CHAFFEE is president of Mayville State University and of Valley City State University in North Dakota. She is a former associate commissioner of higher education in North Dakota.

PETER T. EWELL is senior research associate with the National Center for Higher Education Management Systems (NCHEMS).

KENT M. KEITH, former president of Chaminade University in Hawaii, is an attorney in Hawaii.

WILLIAM G. TIERNEY is professor and director of the Center for Higher Education Policy Analysis, School of Education, at the University of Southern California.

JON F. WERGIN is professor of Education at Virginia Commonwealth University.

INDEX